DEFENDING THE
DIGITAL FRONTIER

DEFENDING THE DIGITAL FRONTIER

A SECURITY AGENDA

Mark W. Doll
Sajay Rai
Jose Granado

JOHN WILEY & SONS, INC.

Published by John Wiley & Sons, Inc., Hoboken, New Jersey.
Published simultaneously in Canada.

Restrict, Run, Recover^{SM} is a servicemark of EYGN Limited.

For general information on our other products and services, or technical support, please contact our Customer Care Department within the United States at 800-762-2974, outside the United States at 317-572-3993 or fax 317-572-4002.

Wiley also publishes its books in a variety of electronic formats. Some content that appears in print may not be available in electronic books.

For more information about Wiley products, visit our Web site at www.wiley.com.

ISBN 0-471-22144-9

Printed in the United States of America.

10 9 8 7 6 5 4 3 2 1

Contents

List of Figures and Tables

Foreword

Defending the Digital Frontier has been written to assist executives in the United States and beyond in understanding the critical nature of security within their organizations. While the focus of the book is digital security, which affects most if not all areas of business today, the book lays out an agenda for addressing a number of critical security risks, issues, and solutions.

Over the past year, President Bush has initiated a major effort to restructure the government and its agencies charged with supporting the homeland security of the United States. These plans, which streamline the chain of command and vastly increase the focus on security within both the federal government and the private sector, will greatly enhance America's ability to detect and mitigate threats and, when necessary, react to security incidents. The President's plans will bring a much needed comprehensive crisis management system to the federal government, including a structure for planning, preparing, and continuously practicing for security threats.

The time has come for senior executives of U.S. corporations to follow the President's lead and make security a mainstream, business critical, board-level issue—something it has not often been.

Like the federal government, senior executives must structure their organizations to address security threats. In most cases, organizations must create a new centralized framework that enables them to assess, design, plan, and implement security solutions for possible threats. Once organizations have taken these steps, they must continue to reevaluate their security posture through ongoing planning, preparation, and practice. This is a new era for American business. It calls for a new approach—a more secure approach. Corporate America's actions will in turn aid in the effort to secure America's homeland and in particular the critical infrastructure on which our economy, citizens, and governments rely.

This is not a situation that can be solved just by increasing corporate security budgets. In the past, security has been relegated to a line item on a balance sheet. Only if evidence of immediate return or the avoidance of serious financial exposure was evident would action be taken to secure the corporate infrastructure. From financial institutions to the energy, utility, healthcare, chemical, and transportation industries, American corporations are vulnerable. That means America is vulnerable.

Historically, many corporate security decisions, even for major organizations, are made not by senior executives, but by people with technical knowledge limited to their areas of expertise. Although they are no doubt dedicated to their responsibilities, they often have too little perspective to consider the impact of their decisions on the entire organization, and in turn upon America's critical infrastructure. The time when security-related decisions could be left to persons at the mid-manager level or decided solely upon budgetary consideration has passed. Senior executives must now take the steps to plan, prepare, and practice to address their organizational security threats and challenges.

Corporate security can only be improved if senior executives demonstrate commitment to the safety and security of their company, its assets, and its people. They must quickly assess the major security issues and the solutions available to address them. Business leaders across all industries must centralize their knowledge, standardize their response to incidents, and properly coordinate their efforts with one another and with all levels of government. It is integral that digital and physical security, crisis management, and business continuity be addressed as one strategic initiative.

The charge of securing corporate America falls upon its business leaders. This book, offered by Ernst & Young and written by Mark Doll, Sajay Rai, and Jose Granado, is not only timely, but comprehensive in outlook and broad in scope. It addresses many of the critical security issues facing corporate America today and should be read by responsible senior management.

THE HONORABLE RUDOLPH W. GIULIANI

Preface

The idea of a frontier brings to mind many images, all of which involve exploration, high risks, and high returns. The concept of a *digital frontier* adds another dimension of uncertainty because it is intangible. The means of getting to the digital frontier—the *hardware*—is the only tangible control associated with it. Everything else—the *data*, the *functions*, and, in the near future, the *means of distribution*—is, for the most part, without a fixed form. The digital frontier as we will define it has no territory and no outer limit other than that existing in the corporate imagination. Protecting the digital frontier is perhaps the greatest challenge facing business organizations in the early part of this millennium because digital security—the protection of *all* components of the digital frontier, including the human component—is complex, costly, and generally misunderstood.

The definition of digital security is amorphous because it affects so many aspects of daily life, yet it rarely produces the measurable return on investment realized by other information-related technologies; therefore, it is frequently ignored or devalued. However, in today's interconnected economy, digital security is a central, if not critical, element of business operations. Having in place a digital security program means an organization has chosen an integrated approach to protecting all of its digital assets: data, the media on which that data is stored, the devices used to create and store the data, and the medium or mode of transporting the data. It also means that the organization has chosen to protect the lives and livelihoods of the employees who use those digital assets in the course of day-to-day operations, to protect the mutual business interests of its customers and suppliers who rely on the availability and integrity of those digital assets, and to maintain the trust of its shareholders and the public who, for any number of reasons, must rely on the organization to preserve and protect the confidentiality of personal data. The consequences of failing to implement measures to protect digital assets can range from merely annoying to life-threatening. The magnitude of these consequences will only compound with the passage of time and the advent of new technologies.

Incidents over the past decade, whether successful or threatened, have highlighted the vulnerability of organizations to technological menace. For example, the Y2K fault, and the Code Red, Nimda, and I Love You worms failed to produce the information holocaust many security experts predicted. However, these threats caused damage estimated in the billions of dollars in downtime, loss of productivity, and repair and recovery efforts and affected almost every company in the United States and many more around the world. According to *Computer Economics*, the worldwide economic impact of the Nimda, Code Red, and Sircam attacks totaled $4.4 billion. The I Love You worm in 2000 inflicted an estimated $8.75 billion in damage worldwide, and, in 1999 the combined impact of the Melissa and Explorer attacks was $2.12 billion.[1] Affected organizations suffered real injuries in terms of money, image, and public confidence; however, the destruction was contained, mitigated, and even deflected in proportion to the effectiveness of the security measures companies had in place. The failure of such threats to cause even greater widespread destruction can be interpreted as a corollary to achieving a measurable return on investment in digital security.

To achieve the highest possible level of digital security, every member of an organization's executive management must realize that digital security is "baked in," not "painted on." Decision makers at that level must understand the need for digital security. Furthermore, they need a basic understanding of digital security and how it can be implemented within their organization. To that end, this book is intended to deconstruct digital security for executive management. It addresses the common problems of information protection for business organizations and it provides a framework in which to analyze and discuss digital security. It offers insight into the technologies, organizational issues, and processes that drive digital security and presents a set of mechanisms for identifying and managing risk to an organization's assets and people.

However, achieving and then defending security at the digital frontier requires more than just informed decision making at the top level. It also depends on the willingness of the executive management to change the organizational mind-set to a security orientation. A security-minded organization will be a secure organization. In this book, we describe what we consider to be the significant risks to an organization's digital security structure and explain why that structure's success relies as heavily on the organization and its people and processes as on technology. We offer a definition of world-class digital security and provide in-depth examples of what we consider to be its six key characteristics: It must be aligned, enterprise-wide, continuous, proactive, validated, and formal.[2] We describe how digital security can be achieved by designing it according to a detailed, proven, three-part Security Agenda: Restrict, Run, and Recover.[SM 3] We detail the nine items that comprise the agenda, which together enable any organization to achieve world-class digital security:

1. Intrusion and virus detection
2. Incident response
3. Privacy
4. Policies, standards, and guidelines
5. Physical security
6. Asset management
7. Entitlement management
8. Vulnerability management
9. Business continuity

We explain why digital security is no longer merely a technical function but a risk management operation requiring executive sponsorship, and is therefore dependent on a fluid strategy centered on identification and mitigation at the highest levels. Finally, we provide an approach for crafting, implementing, and supporting a pervasive security culture that is based on dynamic responsiveness in an evolving environment.

By strengthening the collective digital security knowledge base within an organization from the top down and enabling a clear understanding of the benefits of a comprehensive, inclusive, ongoing security agenda, every organization can build a secure future to the edge of the digital frontier.

MARK W. DOLL

San Jose, California
November 2002

Acknowledgments

We would like to thank two people without whom this book would not have been completed: Stephen L. Bates, contributing author, whose experience, keen insight, extensive knowledge of security, and many hours of research significantly contributed to the content and influenced the concepts in this book; and Mary A. Giery-Smith, technical writer, whose wordsmithing skills, editorial expertise, and ability to express technical concepts in a cogent, accessible fashion brought clarity to our message and enhanced the content of this book.

We would also like to thank the many others whose assistance was invaluable: Tikhon Ferris for his perspectives on IT risk management; Mark Moore, Scott Blanchette, and Gary Lorenz, who provided the shape of the book and much of the content presented in earlier drafts; Robert M. Roberge and Jeffrey L. Gill for their focus on a consistent security message; Christine Sharp for her efficiency and responsiveness as she assisted with graphics and tables; Sherry Flores, for all of her work behind the scenes to keep things organized and running smoothly; the other members of the 350 partners and staff of the Security & Technology Solutions practice of Ernst & Young LLP, whose support and encouragement added greatly to the success of this effort; and Debra Englander at John Wiley & Sons for her patience as this project came together.

M.W.D.

PART ONE
The Challenge of the Frontier

America has always been a land of frontiers that have been continually pushed, reshaped, and then pushed again. Since the evolution of America as a nation, we have been characterized by a restlessness and an unquenchable desire to discover, to tame and to lead. When the first European settlers arrived on America's eastern shore, they had no idea of the vastness of the land that lay before them. Even so, they migrated westward, secure in the knowledge that their collective future held enormous bounties as well as enormous risks. Later settlers, the pioneers who settled the American West, had a better but still incomplete understanding of both the risks and the rewards of redefining this young nation's frontiers.

The overwhelming majority of today's business organizations have invested enthusiastically in the promises of technological advances and have reaped the benefits of productivity gains. As they entered the twenty-first century, these organizations were firmly entrenched in the digital age by virtue of having achieved a high degree of reliance on information technology (IT). Some organizations rushed to the edge of the digital age, to its very frontier, and have become leaders by adopting and utilizing the latest technologies and achieving a high degree of reliance on them. Other firms closely followed these early adopters; others trailed much farther behind.

Despite the widespread use and reliance on new technology, however, this vast new frontier is just as unevenly explored as the American West of the 1800s. Some areas of information technology, such as mainframe security, are well established; the risks are understood and have been addressed. Newer technologies, although heavily relied upon by organizations and their employees, customers, and suppliers as part of the daily routine, nevertheless contain inherent risks that are less well understood by the average user. Examples of these technologies are e-mail systems, the Internet and World Wide Web, and private networks. These technologies have become essential elements of everyday life in corporate America and, indeed, in the global economy.

Just as the familiar laws and infrastructures in the young cities of the American West provided some comfort to nineteenth-century settlers, twenty-first century businesses have found comfort in knowing that somewhere within their organization an IT department has implemented little-understood security countermeasures to protect the organization's information assets from hackers and other malcontents. However, this sort of thinking is naïve. The digital frontier is dynamic; it continues to expand. In many cases, if not most, it has already expanded beyond the ability of organizations to protect themselves from real threats. The security capabilities of companies at the digital frontier should have expanded at the same rate or faster to provide comprehensive protection, but they have not.

When the western pioneers left the cities for the wilderness, more than just the landscape changed. The risks changed. So, too, for today's business organizations. The digital frontier is as unsettled as the frontier faced by America's expansionist settlers with two stark differences: The digital frontier is not a territory on a map, and there is no law of the land.

The digital frontier is virtual and borderless. There are no common rules of engagement that will protect its pioneers, and the standards for recourse or redress are just as inconsistent. However, underlying these differences is one striking similarity between the frontiers that has remained unchanged for more than a century. It is the problem of how to prepare to face things that cannot be predicted or even imagined. Firms that want to reap the benefits of being at the digital frontier—increased productivity, market dominance, and increased customer satisfaction—must be prepared to defend their assets and their people against a variety of security threats that may strike without warning, and may leave little room for recourse other than retrenchment.

Part One describes the challenges facing the most senior stakeholders in the global economy—executive management—whose decisions about digital security today will produce effects that will be felt for years to come. The first two chapters provide an in-depth discussion of how an organization can determine its position with regard to the digital security frontier and an overview of the key characteristics of digital security. The third chapter addresses the issue of resource allocation, including personnel, and provides a context for executing the critical technologies, organizational enhancements, and necessary processes that will enable a firm to achieve digital security. Together, these chapters present the foundation of a cyclical strategy to successfully defend an organization's stake in the digital frontier.

1

The Security Frontier

I n the introduction to Part One, the digital frontier was described as virtual, borderless, and highly dynamic. By implication, its environment is fluid rather than concrete, and transitory rather than fixed. Although such terms lend understanding in the abstract, they are less helpful when trying to quantify the frontier. Therefore, we offer the following operational definition of the digital frontier: *It is the forward edge of technological impact with respect to organizations' usage of technology and their reliance upon it for day-to-day operations to achieve marketable productivity improvements* (see Figure 1.1).

It is important to understand the difference between the "bleeding edge" of technology and the digital frontier because, although they have similarities in terms of their positions at the forefront of innovations with respect to the majority of business organizations, there are several significant distinctions. Companies investing in so-called bleeding edge technologies have as one of their drivers the adoption of the latest technology for experimental purposes. Companies investing to the edge of the digital frontier are careful to adopt the latest and best technology available *with regard to its utility and performance because usage and adoption are critical to productivity gain.*

Just as settlers pushing the boundaries of the American West redrew the maps to show later explorers where the old frontiers had ended and

FIGURE 1.1 The Digital Frontier

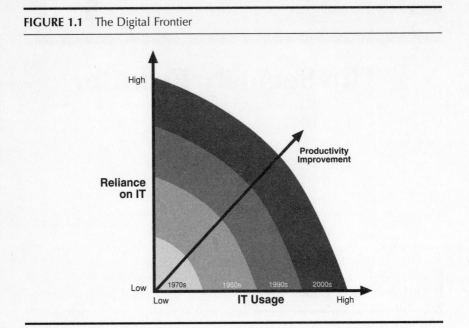

which areas were still open for development, Figure 1.2 shows the four clearly distinguishable eras on the continuum of digital technology. These eras are defined by their architecture, and all were pushed forward by the companies whose executive management understood that there must be a direct correlation between digital investment and operational productivity. Those executive managers knew that a high degree of both usage and reliance is what puts an organization squarely in the digital frontier, and their companies are the ones that traditionally have and are still holding the competitive advantage in the marketplace. The eras shown in Figure 1.2 can be described as follows:

1. *Mainframe:* This era is characterized by highly centralized systems and closed architecture. This era was the advent of the digital age, beginning with the development and use of the Electronic Numerical Integrator and Computer (ENIAC) in 1947.

FIGURE 1.2   Computing Eras That Have Shaped the Digital Frontier

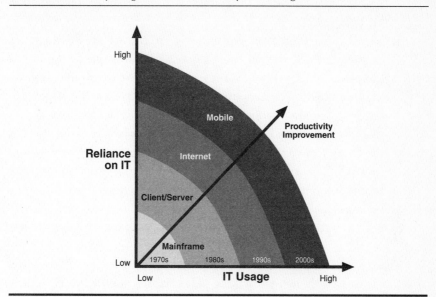

Mainframe systems evolved, but continued to be the platforms of choice until the mid-1980s.

2. *Client/server:* This second major shift along the digital frontier ushered in the concept of distributed information, private users, and decentralized systems. This has proved to be an enduring structure and is still in widespread use today, with adaptations for more advanced technology.

3. *Internet:* The concept of a highly decentralized, open-architecture system that connected widely distributed users had been in use for a decade or more in the form of the original Advanced Research Projects Agency Network (ARPANet) of the U.S. Department of Defense, which connected academic and military research institutions. However, in the 1990s, this network was opened for public access and its usage increased exponentially. By the end of that decade, reliance upon it had become ubiquitous for business

and non-business-related usage. Companies that had previously lagged behind in terms of technological innovation went online in the 1990s.

4. *Mobile:* The fourth wave of innovation, the effects of which are beginning to be felt in the business world at the beginning of the twenty-first century, is the era of wireless communication via highly decentralized, open-architecture systems. This technology is reshaping the digital frontier as wireless technology segues from being at the bleeding edge of technological innovation to the leading edge of the digital frontier. Organizations have begun to study its utility and determine their potential to become reliant upon it. The key factor in how ubiquitous this technology becomes will be its ability to significantly increase productivity without increasing risks to the organization's security framework.

The greatest danger facing organizations that exist at the digital frontier is one of their own making. The last decade of the twentieth century saw an explosion of development in high technology. Microprocessors allowed information to be created, stored, sorted, and reassembled at speeds measured in nanoseconds, and fiber-optic technology enabled that information to be transferred literally at the speed of light. The time lapse between generations of the microchip decreased from being measured in years to being measured in months. Portability became an issue, and the convenience of independent, interconnected desktop workstations was surpassed by laptops, which were in turn surpassed by smaller, sleeker notebook computers. By the end of the century, powerful computers with nearly full functionality fit in a shirt pocket.

Nearly every industry underwent a dramatic evolution as new technologies helped to streamline productivity and increase efficiency. These technological advances fostered a dramatic surge in spending as businesses of every size and description invested heavily in upgrading their IT systems. The ability to digitize information had truly revolutionized the way companies conducted business. Increased usage and increased reliance were viewed as part of a reward cycle that would yield higher productivity and lower associated costs. However, with the precision lent by hindsight, we can now view this behavior by companies at the edge of the digital frontier from the perspective of risk rather than reward. Consideration of the situation from this viewpoint reveals that the closer a company is to the edge of the digital frontier, the greater the probability of failure of the systems relied upon, and the greater the impact of that failure when it occurs. This is *security risk* (see Figure 1.3).

When an organization's security risk (probability and potential impact of failure) is superimposed on productivity (an organization's usage of and reliance on technology), a new frontier emerges. We call this the *security frontier* (see Figure 1.4). Its parameters are measurable, and they are different for every company; therefore, defining it is not difficult. Defending it, however, is nearly impossible.

FIGURE 1.3   Security Risk

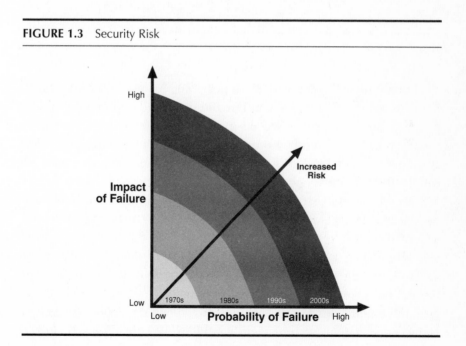

FIGURE 1.4   The Security Frontier

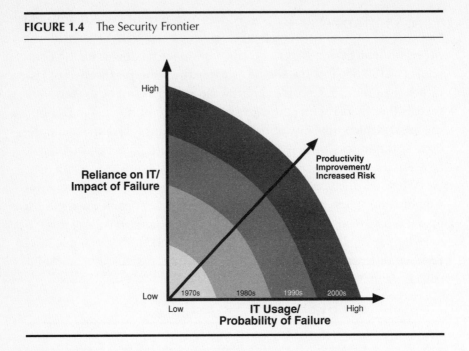

Caught up in the enthusiasm for becoming "wired" in the late 1990s, few companies stopped to consider the consequent vulnerabilities of opening their formerly closed information systems. Even fewer spent proportionally on defending themselves against attacks. This exuberant spending and unintended shortsightedness coalesced to form what we call the *digital security gap* (see Figure 1.5).

The challenges associated with the digital frontier must be identified, acknowledged, and managed in order for organizations to defend against them while maintaining their position at the frontier's leading edge. Defending the digital frontier requires that organizations encourage an evolution within their digital security programs. Detailed descriptions of this evolution are discussed in Chapter 3 and Chapter 8. However, the foundations of this evolution are among the largest challenges facing organizations at the security frontier and are discussed in the following sections.

FIGURE 1.5   The Digital Security Gap

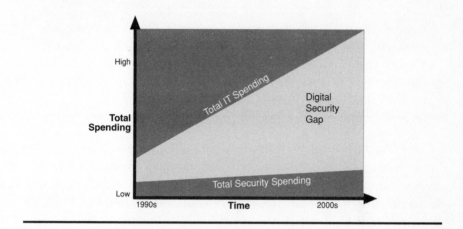

IDENTIFYING THE SECURITY FRONTIER

Meeting the dual challenge of remaining at the edge of the digital frontier while closing an organization's digital security gap requires an understanding of what being at the digital frontier means to the organization, as well as an awareness of how the organization can defend its position there. It means executives should know everything they can about their organization's security frontier and what risks their organization faces. However, nobody can provide that information. To be completely secure, to be completely safe, the executive management of an organization must know what they can't possibly know.

An ***information asset*** is information possessed by an organization during the process of conducting business. The information may be owned by the organization, for example, customer lists, or it may be information placed under the custodianship of the organization for a specified period of time, for example, a credit card number provided by a customer to complete a business transaction.

A **digital asset** is information stored or processed on or by digital media and the corresponding physical and logical devices used for storage, processing, or transport. Examples of digital assets include computer hardware and software, computer hard drives and the data stored on them, and a network and the range of a wireless hub. Digital assets must hold some level of value to stakeholders or be governed by a law or regulation in order to be classified as assets.

Eliminating all threats to and vulnerabilities affecting an organization's digital assets is impossible as well as impractical, just as it is impossible and impractical to secure a nation's borders by building a perimeter so secure that it impedes the flow of commerce. However, securing those assets is both possible and practical. Achieving digital security, much like achieving national security, becomes an exercise in identifying, mitigating, and tracking threats and vulnerabilities and repairing breaches. The work is cyclical and continual, and in order to engage in it effectively, executive management must know what information assets are at risk and understand the organization's current digital security requirements, as well as its current digital security capabilities.

Environment

The digital frontier can be entered unknowingly. Upgrading a system or adding new technologies or components can initiate movement along the digital technology continuum, introducing significant risk to an organization's digital security. A broad understanding of the firm's digital information assets and operations is required in order to determine where an organization exists at the frontier; this knowledge will enable the organization to identify and mitigate that risk. The first step in facing the challenge of the digital frontier is to *determine where an organization is with regard to the security frontier.*

Identification of an organization's position relative to the security frontier involves more than just knowing the basic foundation of its computing resources in terms of usage and reliance. There must be a detailed understanding of why the organization occupies that position on the frontier. Specifically, senior management must understand which assets are being protected and why. What are the issues or requirements driving the organization's utilization and reliance on digital technology? What are the current capabilities of the digital security program in place?

The criticality and sensitivity of information assets may be, but are not necessarily, correlated.

Sensitive information assets are those that could, if compromised, pose grave threats to the organization. Examples of sensitive information include unannounced strategic decisions, human resources information, or intellectual property, such as research and development data.

Critical information assets are those upon which the organization relies to conduct routine business, for instance, to generate revenue and facilitate communications or transactions and could include sensitive and nonsensitive information. An example of critical but not sensitive information would be sales tax information for a retailer— information that is critical to running the business, but the release of which will not compromise the organization.

What information is worthy of protection? Does all of an organization's information require the same level of protection? Where is the most important information stored? For instance, is an organization's most critical or sensitive information stored in databases created using shrinkwrapped applications? Which version of the software is being used, and are all the copies licensed? Is the software installed on one server, or twenty? In which office or offices are the servers located? Who owns the database, and who determines who gets access to the data in it? How frequently is it backed up and where are those backups stored? These are questions that the IT personnel in an organization should be able to answer quickly. But do those IT specialists understand the value of the information? Should they? Should IT be the only repository of that information?

The identification of information assets is one element of understanding where an organization exists with regard to the security frontier. This identification must involve the IT department, certainly, but it is also a function that must be understood and undertaken by management at the highest levels. After all, implementing every high-technology security precaution available cannot prevent unauthorized access to a sensitive database stored on a remote server if no one is aware that the server exists. This is why comprehensive asset identification must be addressed with the same gravity as is given to an organization's security capabilities and its security requirements when planning to deploy a digital security program.

The second part of the asset identification issue is understanding who or what sets up the security issues. In other words, how are an organization's digital security requirements determined? Is an organization bound to comply with federal security regulations, including privacy regulations?[1] Do business partners impose specific technical security configurations on an organization's external networks? What would be the impact of an unintended release of sensitive or critical information?

Privacy is the right of an individual to determine to what degree he or she is willing to disclose personal or other information about him- or herself. When such information is provided to other entities, individuals, or organizations, this right extends to the collection, distribution, and storage of that information.

Every organization has its own mix of regulatory-, industry-, and internally driven digital security mandates; therefore, the answers to these questions are key to determining an organization's digital security requirements. Typically, external mandates can be obtained from clearly defined sources. Within the healthcare industry, for example, the security and privacy of patient information are addressed by the Healthcare Insurance Portability and Accountability Act (HIPAA) of 1996 and other federal and state regulatory requirements. Similarly, in the banking and financial industries, the Gramm Leach Bliley (GLB) Act of 1999 and other regulations set requirements to protect customer information.[2] Internally driven requirements are typically less clearly defined, and frequently organizations must initiate far-ranging audits or assessments to determine them. Once understood, these mandates can serve as a foundation for determining digital security objectives and as a framework for measuring how well those objectives are being met.

Examples of Federal Laws Impacting Security Considerations

- Patriot Act of 2001
- Digital Privacy Act of 2000
- Electronic Communications Privacy Act of 1986, 2000
- Gramm Leach Bliley (GLB) Act of 1999
- Electronic Freedom of Information Act of 1996
- Healthcare Insurance Portability and Accountability Act (HIPAA) of 1996
- National Information Infrastructure Protection Act of 1996
- Computer Security Act of 1987
- Computer Fraud and Abuse Act of 1986
- Computer Crime Control Act of 1984
- Privacy Act of 1974

Once the critical and/or sensitive information has been identified and the security mandates for protecting those assets are understood, the state of an organization's existing security capabilities must be considered. What does that firm's digital security program look like today? For instance, how is the network monitored with regard to unauthorized access? What is the process for providing new personnel with user access to Internet applications? What is the security configuration for the payroll application? Who has been given responsibility, direction, and authority to perform digital security functions? Most importantly, could the models on which the answers are based be considered best-in-class?

Responsibilities

For each of the past seven years, the Computer Security Institute (CSI) and the Federal Bureau of Investigation (FBI) have surveyed large U.S.

corporations, government agencies, and financial, medical, and academic organizations about digital security issues. The results are published as the annual *CSI/FBI Computer Crime and Security Survey.* One of the more chilling statistics presented in the survey is that of the 98 percent of respondents that have World Wide Web sites, 21 percent *did not know* whether there had been unauthorized access to or misuse of their site in the preceding 12 months.[3] Although it is inappropriate, this lack of understanding is not surprising. However, it is inexcusable for an organization operating at the digital frontier; in the near future it may be actionable. That is why the second step in identifying an organization's security frontier is to *define executive management's responsibilities* with regard to defending the organization's position at the digital frontier.

IT governance refers to the oversight and guidance of information and applied technology within the business and business-related fields by stakeholders, which can include an organization's directors and senior management, as well as process owners and IT suppliers, and users, and auditors.
                    —Board Briefing on IT Governance, IT Governance Institute

---

Management responsibilities for digital security are but one component of corporate responsibilities for IT governance. According to the IT Governance Institute, which provides guidance on current and future issues pertaining to IT governance,[4] the responsibility for IT governance lies with the board of directors and executive management. Such governance "is an integral part of the enterprise governance and consists of the leadership and organizational structures and processes that ensure that the organization's IT sustains and extends the organization's strategies and objectives."[5] Specifically, management must address "[t]he risks of doing business in an interconnected digital world and the dependence on entities beyond the direct control of the enterprise; IT's impact on business continuity due to increasing reliance on information and IT in all aspects of the enterprise"; and, "[t]he failures of IT," which are having an increasing impact on reputation and enterprise value.[6]

In today's global, digitally-linked marketplace, executive management has a fiduciary responsibility to shareholders as well as a responsibility to the organization. The latter responsibility is operational in nature—to ensure the continuation of business in the face of threats and attacks. It is the responsibility of executive management to deploy a digital security program that enables management to determine which risks to accept, which risks to mitigate, and which resources to deploy toward that mitigation. Carrying out these responsibilities entails the following:

- Setting the objectives for digital security.
- Allocating resources for a program to achieve and maintain digital security, including monitoring and measuring the program itself.
- Promoting a digital security culture.
- Reducing the total risk of security failures while eliminating high-impact events.
- Conceiving a charter for the digital security program that establishes goals and standards for an implementation framework.

Priorities

The nature of threats and vulnerabilities at the digital frontier will be discussed later in this chapter. However, any attack at the frontier can be guaranteed to have two characteristics: speed and severity. When a firm's information system is successfully attacked, whether the attack is made to its networks, its website, or any other subsystem, more than just information is compromised. Trust has been lost at every level. An organization's structure, its internal culture, and its corporate image are affected, and the repercussions may be most strongly felt with regard to consumer confidence and in turn, on the bottom line. Therefore, the third step in facing the challenge of the digital frontier is to *define executive management's priorities* in defending an organization's position at the frontier.

Earlier in this chapter, information was introduced regarding an organization's digital security requirements and capabilities, and how best to identify its digital information assets. This section raises the same issues but from a management perspective. For instance, what is the real threat to an organization under or facing an attack? What will be the direct, immediate business impacts of a release of sensitive or critical information? Will all means of entry to the system have to be shut down? If so, for how long? What is the intended target of the attack? What can be compromised in an attack: shareholder and consumer confidence, brand image, share price, or safety of personnel? Which assets are controlled by systems, and what would be the effect of the failure of those systems? Is the organization security-minded? Who in the organization understands the technology? What are the options with regard to defense? How fast is fast enough when you're talking about responding to a breach of security? How much is enough to spend defending an organization's position at the digital frontier? What is the return on investment of implementing security measures?

Executive management's priorities are found in the answers to these questions. The challenge lies in determining what to do *before* a crisis strikes, and then doing it continuously. This necessitates an entire organization adopting a security mind-set. It also requires that executive managers learn more than just the technical terminology of an organization's digital security program; they must have at least a basic understanding of what digital security means, what it involves, and what such a program can and cannot achieve. The less executive managers understand about both the technology and the solutions, the more *unwarranted* decision-making power they may be placing in the hands of technical people whose scope may be limited with regard to an organization's goals and needs. This delegation of authority to persons who may not understand the business risk versus the business return is inappropriate, and possibly dangerous.

There are no "right" answers to the questions asked in this chapter. The responses will vary for every organization depending on the industry, the product or products produced by the organization, the organization's reliance on technology, and the type of technology in use by the organization. Therefore, the priorities for every organization will be different, as will the options available to them in the planning stages. The goal, however, should be the same: to build a digital security program.

CHALLENGES AT THE FRONTIER

Information has always possessed an inherent value. As a result, information security is not a new phenomenon. Evidence suggests that information protection is nearly as old as civilized society. Ancient Egyptians, Greeks, and Romans demonstrated varying degrees of encryption and decryption expertise in an effort to keep sensitive information secret. Although the practice of protecting information from unauthorized access, modification, or compromise has changed little over time, the methodology has changed dramatically.

Many traditional barriers to information exchange do not exist in today's business environment. Access to sensitive data no longer requires physical proximity; data exists in smaller spaces and can be stored on increasingly compact, easily transportable media and can be transferred by wireless means. The benefits of speed and portability are balanced by the knowledge that information is more accessible and less protected than ever before. The rush to continually extend the boundaries of the digital frontier, to meet increasingly aggressive operational objectives in shorter periods of time, has left many business organizations in the precarious position of having more information assets open to compromise than ever before as they try to retrofit their existing digital security apparatus and countermeasures to meet today's security needs.

Threats and Vulnerabilities

Once an organization has identified its place at the digital frontier and executive management has defined its responsibilities and priorities with regard to defending that place, there is still a group of unknowns to consider. The unknowns in this case are a loose collection of issues called *threats* and *vulnerabilities*. Threats to and vulnerabilities of an organization's digital security program are two sides of the same coin. Both are capable of inflicting extreme damage, and both may be effectively deflected with prescriptive vigilance and reactive diligence.[7]

Four Broad Categories of Threats

- *Interception:* Data is siphoned from the system.
- *Interruption:* Networks and Internet access are rendered unusable in a denial-of-service attack.
- *Modification:* Authorizations or access codes are changed.
- *Fabrication:* False information is inserted into a system.

A threat to an information system is any act upon or against the system that is performed with the intention to cause harm. Threats can be internal or external to the organization; they can include human threats, such as disgruntled employees, or they may be derived from vulnerabilities, such as a remote server no one is aware of. *Vulnerabilities are generally inherent weaknesses in an information system,* although some vulnerabilities may result from deliberate acts or omissions. Despite peer review, little commercial software reaches the market free from vulnerabilities, and even systems developed in-house frequently achieve full-scale implementation prior to the detection of potential vulnerabilities. Potential avenues of attack are discovered almost daily, and such information is freely disseminated among the IT community and other interested parties, including potential intruders or hackers.

Common Causes of Information System Vulnerabilities

- A developer's risk-versus-reward analysis.
- Development efforts that focus on performance rather than security.
- A systems designer's inability to predict potential targets for exploitation.
- Inefficient change control.
- The average user's misperceptions about security risks.
- Misunderstandings about security protocols and the need for them.

According to the 2002 CSI/FBI Survey, "the threat from computer crime and other information security breaches continues unabated and the financial toll is mounting."[8] Ninety percent of the survey's respondents had detected computer security breaches within the 12 months preceding the survey, and 80 percent acknowledged financial losses due to those breaches.[9] The 44 percent of respondents that were willing or able to quantify their losses reported an aggregate $455 million worth of damage.[10] The most serious areas of loss were the theft of proprietary information, which totaled $170 million, and financial fraud, which totaled $115 million. The highest individual loss due to theft of proprietary information was $50 million; the average loss was $6.57 million.[11] The highest individual loss due to financial fraud was also $50 million; the average loss was $4.6 million.[12] Insider abuse of Internet access, for example, employees' use of company computers or access to download pornography or pirated software, or the inappropriate use of the organization's e-mail system, cost respondents $50 million.[13] Despite a high proportion of antivirus software implementation, viruses and their aftermath were detected by 85 percent of respondents and carried a price tag of $49.9 million.[14]

As this information shows, the risks are real and the stakes are high. It is incumbent upon the executive management team to understand what they are facing as they stand at the edge of the digital frontier. An organization operating at the security frontier must understand that its place is a dangerous one. It has a landscape that changes, and with each incremental change, everything changes. This means that although any group or system within the organization can be the component leading the organization into the frontier, that component may be the vulnerable area, or it may cause a vulnerability to be overlooked. All it takes is one person who doesn't "get it" to cause a security breach that can take vast amounts of time, money, and manpower to fix and that can have grave repercussions in the marketplace.

There are obstacles beyond threats and vulnerabilities that present challenges for organizations at the edge of the digital frontier. Many of these obstacles are the product of misperceptions that can influence organizations in many ways, permeate the decision cycle from the executive to the user level, and undermine security efforts. Examples of these misperceptions include:

- Information security efforts are an IT domain, or the purview of a specialized security group.
- Security threats and vulnerabilities are unique to high-profile industries or companies.
- Outsiders compromise information most frequently, and such compromise is often detected and prosecuted.[15]
- Security policies are sufficient to guide operations in a secure manner.
- Security technology will solve security needs.
- Security impairs organizational objectives and serves as a barrier to progress.

An Attack Scenario

Many threats exist on the digital frontier. Unfortunately, many companies have digital security programs that may be, in themselves, a serious vulnerability with regard to their ability to identify threats and address vulnerabilities in a way that mitigates the impact of digital security incidents, and their ability to respond appropriately when an attack occurs. Consider the following real-world scenario and some of the questions it raises from the perspective of an executive who thought the organization was secure.

Stage One: Onset and Initial Response

An employee who has been with a major healthcare services firm for 15 years leaves the company under less than pleasant circumstances. Shortly thereafter, her former coworkers and others complain that their passwords on certain corporate systems, such as e-mail, are no longer working. It is known that the ex-employee had knowledge of those systems, including default or known passwords, and there are indications that she has used that knowledge to access components of those systems. In an effort to resolve the situation, IT management issues an urgent request for employees to change their system passwords. Some employees respond appropriately and change their passwords; others ignore the request. At this stage in the scenario, several issues have been raised:

- The organization's policy regarding removing employees from the system when they leave is not being followed, nor is the organization's policy regarding requiring employees to change passwords on a routine schedule.
- The organization's policy regarding the use of corporate applications that rely on default or hard-coded passwords at the system level—in other words, critical application functionality will break if the passwords are changed—has been shown to be a vulnerability, and there is apparently no policy restricting systems from using hard-coded passwords or requiring implementation teams to change default passwords prior to going live with systems.
- The decision to shut down compromised systems or disconnect them from the Internet must be considered. Does current policy indicate the party responsible for making that decision, and does it address the impact of that decision on business?

Stage Two: Information-Gathering and Option Analysis

Because the ex-employee has gained illicit access to the e-mail system, the potential exists that other Internet applications also may have been compromised, such as the firm's online subscriber information database. Some of these applications may have default passwords that are crucial to their operations. The ex-employee may know these default passwords, or she also may know other employees' passwords to these applications. As a response to this potential issue, programmers and vendors for the potentially compromised applications are contacted. They report that changing certain passwords on some systems is possible; however, it will take a month or more to make necessary programming changes and conduct remedial testing. The one-month time frame will affect the availability of the applications—perhaps even requiring that they be taken offline, which would necessitate a public explanation. This time frame will require adjusting the priorities of the current IT staff, thereby affecting the timeline of other projects currently underway.

Meanwhile, system and security administrators have put extra resources into the effort to determine how she is accessing Internet systems, but have little to show for their efforts. Some of the organization's information systems are configured to log activity; others are not. However, even those systems that log information are only logging certain events, for example, failed logins. They offer nothing in this situation because the ex-employee is not failing to log in; she knows passwords and she knows the system's "back doors." She knows where the system's holes are, which means she could change security configurations on the systems and no one would know. This raises the following additional issues:

- There are no implemented policies for logging security events on all systems or for accountability with regard to monitoring those systems.
- Without knowing which systems have been compromised, the organization cannot learn whether data has been modified, stolen, or deleted, or whether sensitive or critical information, such as customer data or information regarding business partners, has been compromised.

Stage Three: Escalation

Five days have elapsed since the first security breach was discovered. The ex-employee is still accessing corporate systems and changing employee passwords. She has hijacked the e-mail account of a current employee and uses it to send an internal e-mail to management. This e-mail, appearing to come from a current employee, complains that the ex-employee was "let go" unfairly and "did nothing wrong." The issues under discussion have become broader in tone, and more urgent:

- Activating the business continuity or disaster recovery plans is considered.

- The decision to contact law enforcement is considered, as well as the public relations ramifications of taking that step.

Stage Four: Malicious Escalation

The ex-employee sends another e-mail to selected company managers; this one contains an agenda. It reveals that for some time she was frustrated by the firm's lack of security and that "no one listened" to her attempts to address it. Now, she has their attention. The e-mail further reveals that she is in possession of patient healthcare histories and intends to disclose the information to the public, just to show how insecure the company's environment is.

At this juncture, the scenario could move in several directions. However, the point has been made that the well-being of the organization has been placed in grave jeopardy by the actions of one person who may have limited but critical knowledge of the system and perhaps only ordinary computer skills. This scenario or one eerily close to it could be played out in any large company in any industry at any given time. Executive-level managers and corporate officers must ask themselves how it would be handled if it happened at their firm:

- Would the digital security program currently in place have the resources to find the necessary answers, and do so in a timely and organized fashion?
- Would prior decisions made by executive management about digital security empower or hinder those responsible for digital security as they sought to find solutions?
- What would it cost to address this scenario?
- What would shutting down a busy web site for 24 hours cost in terms of lost revenue, not to mention the damage to the organization's public image?
- What are the legal ramifications of having sensitive private information publicly released?
- What would it cost to have system administrators spend hundreds of hours investigating the incident and rebuilding compromised systems?

- What would it cost to have administrators and senior management spend dozens or hundreds hours in meetings during and after the incident?
- What would it cost to have the public, government, and media relations departments spend hundreds of hours working on damage control plans and collateral materials intended to restore decreased customer and shareholder confidence?
- How much will the stock price drop, and how long will it take to rebound?
- Worst of all, what if such an attack happens again before the organization has a new program in place?

2

Security Characteristics

Settlers determined to move west in nineteenth-century America had many decisions to make beyond choosing a destination. They had to consider the timing of the trip and its probable duration, the type and quantity of supplies they would need, and which route to take and what sort of weather to expect. They also had to decide whether to move with a large group, believing in safety in numbers, or go with a smaller group, believing that speed would help ensure success. Each group had to determine for itself what degree of risk was acceptable, and apply its own criteria to reach that decision.

The set of decisions facing the executive management of a business organization today is not much different. After an organization's executive management team has identified its position at the digital security frontier, has defined its responsibilities and priorities, and understands the dangers of potential threats and vulnerabilities, its work has just begun. The next step is to define the model of an organization in which the information assets are secured and, using requirements pertinent to the organization's position on the digital frontier, determine how close to that model executives want or need their organization to be.

Constructing and implementing a digital security program that meets the executive management team's definition of leading security practices entails coordination of efforts across a broad spectrum of organizational entities. There are cost factors that must be addressed, including actual expenditures as well as the cost of redirected resources. Time also plays a large role in the effort. Assessing the existing structure, planning and implementing the changes, and training personnel in the new countermeasures and procedures (as well as the new way of thinking about security) all take time.

In this chapter we provide the foundation upon which an organization can begin to plan and then construct a digital security program. This foundation consists of six characteristics that provide the framework for a world-class security program. These characteristics constitute a series of business models that organizations can build into their security systems with the goal maximizing shareholder value by reducing risk and maximizing return. Executive management can use the framework provided by these characteristics to determine how to approach the building of digital security into their business objectives.

ALIGNED

An organization's digital security program must be *aligned*. It must attain and maintain the appropriate alignment between digital security IT organization parameters, digital assets, and business objectives to guarantee focus on the overall objectives of the organization. Many organizations struggle to align digital security to business objectives, and the struggle can frequently be attributed to several factors:

- Justifying security expenditures within traditional return-on-investment models and need-based frameworks has always been difficult, leaving managers responsible for security decisions to make do with existing resources or expand resources in less critical but more visible areas.
- Businesses may not query customers as to the value those customers place on certain security services; therefore, the allocation of existing security resources is focused elsewhere.

- The core business units of the organization and the IT unit may view their objectives—for example, increased productivity and market share for the former and increased performance and security for the latter—as distinct from each other, rather than integrated. This lack of alignment can inhibit the IT unit's ability to achieve its security objective, which is to enable the business units to achieve their objectives while protecting against loss or compromise of information assets.

In most large organizations, business objectives, such as increased productivity and increased market share, are supported by digital assets, for example, customer lists, intellectual capital, supplier profiles, production schedules, and work flow. These digital assets are maintained and supported by the IT department, which traditionally also has responsibility for protecting those assets. The security function, however, is frequently relegated to an off-shoot position on the organizational chart: The security manager might report to middle management within IT, security issues are blended into the larger IT picture, and the importance of the security function becomes diluted. The distance between the top levels of management and the security team, which is also the distance between the organization's business goals and the IT department's protection of those goals, is known as the *security management gap*.

From the perspective of executive management, the security function is a technical one, responsibility for which resides within the IT group. Decisions regarding security policies, practices, or technological improvements are frequently considered "wire and cable" issues and, therefore, best left to the experts: personnel on the technical side of the "security divide." Unfortunately, this delegation of authority places responsibility for important, even critical, strategic decisions, which will significantly affect the utility and convenience of the entire organization's information systems, on someone who may not fully understand the organization's business objectives.

Ignoring this lack of alignment is risky behavior for any organization because advances in technology continually compress the time needed to discover and react to threats. If the security objectives are not aligned directly to the business objectives, the digital security team will not be able to react fast enough when facing a threat or attack because they may not have a full understanding of the risk it poses to the core business. It is incumbent upon top management to become directly involved in security-related policy and risk decisions by having a direct link to the security team. Risks to the business objectives and the possible impact of those risks must be determined by those at the top of the organization, and policy must be set by them as well, after receiving expert input from digital security professionals. Implementation and monitoring can then be delegated to the security team.

> Seventy-nine percent of respondents in the Ernst & Young 2002 Digital Security Overview survey indicated that the documentation, implementation, and follow-through cycle for their information security policies was not being carried out completely.

If, when an organization is upgrading its technology, the executive management brings digital security considerations into their orbit of regard, a security management gap would not develop. However, in the 1990s, extraordinary changes were taking place at the digital frontier and few senior-level managers understood the inherent risks associated with adopting the new Internet technologies. The focus was on improving productivity, and security was considered a secondary, or tertiary, issue. Technology has continued to advance, and the executive management of organizations worldwide is realizing that advances in technology must be balanced with advances in security.

An aligned digital security program is one in which executive management has recognized that digital security is a critical organizational element that enables the business units to maintain productivity gains at the leading edge of the digital frontier. This recognition by executive management of the strategic importance of digital security manifests itself in the form of executive sponsorship. The digital security program realizes this executive sponsorship via direct accountability at the board of directors level, with dotted-line reporting relationships to executive steering committees, and privacy officers. This visible sponsorship effectively places digital security high on the priority list of organizational objectives. When executive management exhibits this level of commitment to digital security, the security program becomes aligned with management and business objectives. In an aligned situation, the flow of communication between the digital security team and executive management is unimpeded—therefore, the message is undiluted. The digital security team can convey information regarding the state of security in the organization directly to executives and, at the same time, executive management can provide direct guidance to the digital security team.

> Within the energy industry, 18 percent of respondents indicated that they "rarely or never" reviewed information security policies for consistency with current business practices and risk strategy. Within the same industry group, 27 percent indicated their policies are reviewed only when a perceived need arises.

The importance of aligning core business objectives with digital security decisions is presented in Figure 2.1. Highly effective digital security programs are found in organizations that recognize the strategic value of attaining and maintaining a high degree of aligned protection for their information assets. The executive management of organizations in which digital security has unimpeded executive-level representation understands that meeting organizational objectives requires integrating the ability to conduct business at a high degree of consistency with the ability to leverage technology to ensure peak performance in all sectors of the business. Managers of digital security programs within these organizations understand the direction established by executive management with regard to digital security policies. Therefore, they can

FIGURE 2.1   An Aligned Digital Security Framework

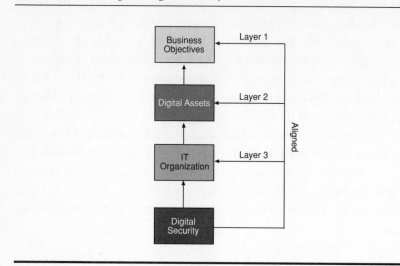

map those policies to the procedures and technologies that enable the program to achieve its prescribed role, which is to protect *all* of the organization's digital assets.

ENTERPRISE-WIDE

An organization's digital security program must be *enterprise-wide*. A successful program takes a holistic view of the security needs for the entire organization, as well as its extended enterprise which includes customers and suppliers, to ensure consistent, efficient deployment. Many organizations can point to one business unit, office, or function that exhibits excellent qualities with regard to digital security. Although that is a good start, it is only a start. Digital security must be considered as an objective in itself because an organization is only as secure as its least secure link. This alone is reason enough for executive management to pay close attention to the concept of enterprise-wide security measures.

Obstacles abound during the planning and implementation phases of deploying an enterprise-wide digital security program, and any one of them can inhibit the program's reach:

- Perhaps the organization has a decentralized structure that has allowed several digital security teams to exist internally, each with a different agenda and level of security expertise, and without a single point of coordination or direction.
- Perhaps digital security policies have not been approved at an enterprise-wide level.
- Perhaps the digital security program that exists has been relegated to a passive, reactive role, or perhaps its manager has no authority to mandate or implement enterprise-wide security.

Enterprise-wide digital security programs share a common critical trait that enables performance at an enterprise level: *authority*. Such programs are sponsored and funded at the executive level, driven by enterprise-wide requirements, directed by executive-approved policy, and are recognized across the enterprise as bearing the responsibility for carrying out digital security. These factors work together to establish the authority for the digital security team to operate an enterprise-wide digital security program.

As Figure 2.2 shows, the concept of enterprise-wide digital security begins at the core of an organization and moves outward in all directions, encompassing not only the organization itself but the second and third generations of organizations on which it depends for secure support and to which it must pledge to provide secure support. Enterprise-wide digital security moves outward from its initial core of the executive management team to include the organization's business units. From there it expands to encompass the organization's markets, which include distributors, buyers, and sellers; the organization's customers and those customers' customers; and the organization's suppliers and those suppliers' suppliers. It extends further still to encompass other stakeholders in security strategies, such as regulatory bodies, for instance the Securities and Exchange Commission (SEC), and federal, state, and local law

FIGURE 2.2   An Enterprise-Wide Digital Security Framework

enforcement. When taken together, these parts constitute a unified front for defense at the digital frontier.

> Eighty-six percent of companies surveyed have intrusion detection systems in place. However of those companies, only 35 percent actively monitor 95 to 100 percent of their *critical* servers for intrusions.

CONTINUOUS

An organization's digital security program must be *continuous*. Real-time monitoring and updating of all security policies, procedures, and processes is critical to ensuring a timely response to issues and opportunities.

One of the difficulties of implementing a comprehensive digital security program is that it must be continuously updated. Not occasionally. Not periodically. Continuously. This presents an enormous challenge to any organization, but it is particularly onerous to organizations whose executive management does not understand the nature of today's technology. In today's globally interconnected world, technology changes on a daily basis. Threats and vulnerabilities can appear and become full-fledged attacks within extremely compressed time frames: days or even hours. Much of the security technology changes in response; preemptive changes are less common.

Inattention to security issues or inappropriate responses to security breaches place organizations at enormous risk of sustaining damage to their brand, their credibility, and their bottom line. In the near future, that list may be expanded to include damage to individuals as Congress and regulatory agencies reassess the role executive managers play in enabling injury to shareholders through lax security practices.

> Forty-six percent of respondents indicated that they use manual or partially automated methods of tracking physical assets as opposed to fully automated methods.

Organizations with heightened awareness of digital security issues change their technology accordingly. However, organizations with world-class security programs in place do more than that—they engage in a continuous cycle of assessing, updating, and redeploying their security program. Such programs adopt a *life cycle* perspective similar to software development life cycles, which incorporate steps from analysis to implementation. The digital security four-stage life cycle can be described as plan, secure, confirm, remediate, as shown in Figure 2.3.

Executive management must coordinate the security objectives (maximal justified protection) with the business objectives (maximal performance utilizing information assets). Once this parallel structure has been established and communicated to the digital security team, the program must be developed and the assets secured. The secured state includes full implementation from a people, processes, and technology perspective. As elements of the security program are in place and

FIGURE 2.3   A Continuous Digital Security Framework

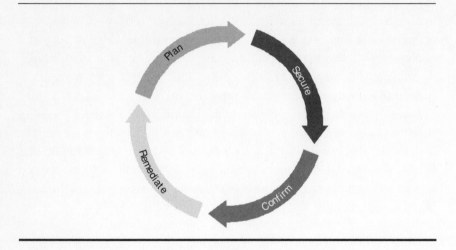

functioning, they must be confirmed independently and as part of the larger system. New or unresolved issues (detected vulnerabilities, threats, procedural or organizational obstacles, etc.) must be addressed and remediated to full, secure functionality.

The next action taken is the most important, and that is to *initiate the cycle again.* Issues discovered during the confirmation process or changes made during the remediation process will have effected change within the overall program and may have created new vulnerabilities. To ignore this step is to render the digital security program static and therefore, ineffectual.

PROACTIVE

An organization's digital security program must be *proactive.* It is imperative that a security program be able to effectively anticipate potential threats and vulnerabilities to maintain the confidentiality, integrity, and availability of information assets. This is an enormous task. It is enormously important. It is enormously misunderstood. Having a proactive program means taking steps to mitigate known or potential risks before they occur *as well as* having in place a plan for responding to an attack. It means paying attention to what makes the organization a potential target, determining what a potential intruder or disgruntled employee might want to damage or destroy, and taking measures to protect those assets before an attack occurs. It means *learning* what the vulnerabilities are, *surveilling* the known points of access for illegitimate activity, and *curtailing* unauthorized activity as soon as it's discovered. The foundation of a proactive approach to digital security is ensuring that the organization has applied enough resources to the digital security program to enable these activities to take place because each of these activities involves in-depth research, planning, and monitoring.

> Only 16 percent of respondents have wide-scale deployment of vulnerability tracking mechanisms and knowledge of all critical information vulnerabilities.

In order to identify impending threats and vulnerabilities, those responsible for digital security must have access to multiple sources of information, both internal and external, and the time to review them. They must determine the validity or accuracy of the information. They must understand how the new threats and vulnerabilities could affect the organization. They must synthesize the information and communicate it to executive management, and they must do all of this quickly in order to be effective. If a digital security program cannot do these things, or cannot do them in a time-effective manner, the program will be forced to operate in a reactive mode.

As shown in Figure 2.4, the traditional approach to digital security was to react to a real or potential threat by increasing organizational defenses, only to allow the readiness to diminish as the threat faded. The next time a threat appeared, the effort required to address it effectively would be as great as it had been the previous time. That model was never cost-efficient; but today, for an organization to allow

FIGURE 2.4   A Proactive Digital Security Framework

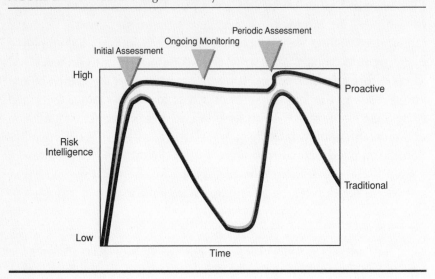

its defenses to languish because no threat is imminent could potentially be considered negligent. Today's threats appear more rapidly and are disseminated through globally-linked systems more quickly than ever before. In today's high-speed, inter-connected world, threats are always imminent; they just may not be easily perceived.

Organizations with highly effective digital security programs understand the value of vulnerability management. Those organizations dedicate resources to this effort and put in place processes that enable a proactive defense against new threats and vulnerabilities and ensure an appropriate response when they surface.

VALIDATED

An organization's digital security program must be *validated*. Achieving world-class digital security requires third-party validation of critical security components. However, it also requires validation of business objectives.

This dual, integrated validation effort enables an organization to confirm that appropriate risk management and mitigation measures are in place.

> According to the Ernst & Young 2002 Digital Security Overview, 66 percent of respondents indicated that their information security policies are not in complete compliance with the domains defined by ISO 17799, CISSP, Common Criteria, or other recognized models.

As mentioned in the discussions of the other key characteristics of a highly effective security program, testing, or validation, is a vital step toward achieving full, effective implementation. There are different levels of validation that apply to different aspects of the organization. The critical factor in determining the necessary level of validation—in other words, the rigor of the test—is the degree of risk that the organization wishes to accept after validation has taken place. The shaded areas in Figure 2.5 represent the need to balance, to some degree, the level

FIGURE 2.5   A Validated Digital Security Framework

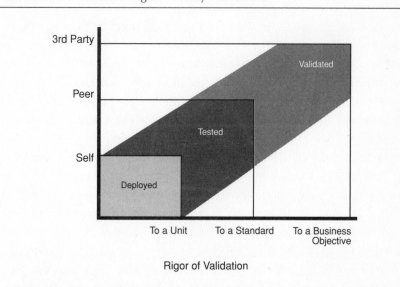

of independence with the rigor of testing to achieve optimal results in the validation efforts. For example, third-party validation to a system unit, without being validated to some standard or business objective, may have limited value compared to that same third-party validation of a system to a given standard or business objective.

As shown in Figure 2.5, situational factors can dictate that internal testing is suitable, for instance if there is a low risk of system failure and/or the impact of that failure presents a tolerable risk. If the system undergoing validation is at the business-unit level, self-testing, or testing by personnel responsible for the system or asset, may be acceptable. This would be the minimum standard for testing. As the level of integration or involvement within the system or with regard to the asset increases, the risk of failure and/or the impact of that failure on the organization increases, as does the need to mitigate risks. This situation must be addressed from a managed-risk approach, which renders unit testing unacceptable but which may not necessitate independent, third-party validation. In such circumstances, it is possible that validation requirements can be met by having independent validation conducted internal to the organization but external to the unit responsible for the system itself.

The third situation presented in Figure 2.5 involves the validation of trusted systems. When the unvalidated system is one that facilitates enterprise-wide productivity or performance, for instance, the e-mail system or critical data networks, the risk of failure increases dramatically as does the impact of that failure. In such a scenario, independent, third-party validation is necessary to ensure the enterprise-wide protection of digital assets at a highly effective level.

As Figure 2.5 illustrates, different levels and methods of validation apply to different components of a digital security system. However, whatever the level or method of validation used, there are two key principles that must be understood in order to effectively understand and utilize the results. The validation process must be *thorough:* Not only must the program itself be validated, but every security component within the program must be validated. The validation process also must be *repeated:* A component or system is validated at a fixed point in time, and changes to any part of the system may invalidate other components or subsystems in ways that are known or unknown.

> Forty-four percent of respondents stated that policy compliance is monitored or administrated in an ad hoc fashion, and 6 percent indicated their policy compliance is neither monitored nor administered.

Each component of an overall business process must be validated as an independent entity and as part of the larger system, application, or combination of technology that supports that business process. Validation must take into account all interfaces or interactions between components, applications, and systems. As each component, or group of components that comprise a business process, undergoes the validation process, the security for that component is enhanced. When each component or group of components is validated cyclically, the security for the entire organization is enhanced. The interval between validation efforts for each component, group of components, or business system will differ, as will the rigor of the validation process, depending on several factors:

- One factor is the maturity of the entity being validated. In the early implementation phase of any component or system, there will likely be more remediable issues detected, requiring more validation cycles than will be necessary when the component or system has been operating for a longer period of time.
- Another factor is number of areas of potential compromise within the component or system. If an organization has 3,000 servers on four continents in 12 offices, testing all of them with any sort of regularity would be beyond the scope of most validation efforts. Therefore, the organization may opt to validate small groups of randomly chosen servers according to a predetermined schedule.
- Another factor is the quantity and type of resources available not only to carry out the validation process, but to follow through with remediation and revalidation.

Implementing a comprehensive, ongoing, tiered validation process that is based on a risk-directed framework will enable an organization to detect and manage vulnerabilities before they become liabilities, which is one more step to achieving world-class security.

FORMAL

An organization's digital security program must be *formal*. Policies, standards, and guidelines, which provide fundamental direction on digital security issues and are endorsed by senior staff, must be documented, tested, and then communicated to every member of the organization.

Conceptually, a formal digital security program seems simple and, in reality, it is. However, the designation *formal,* in this context, requires that a program possess a specific combination of qualities, as shown in Figure 2.6. The figure shows four possible classifications of a digital security program: situational, experience-based, documented, and formal.

A situational program is characterized by minimal documentation of policies, procedures, or processes and minimal or episodic confirmation.

FIGURE 2.6   A Formal Digital Security Framework

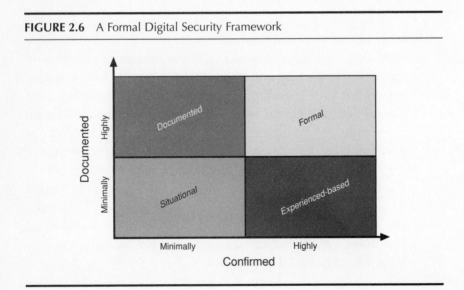

For instance, when a breach of security is discovered, the system is patched; the patch may be tested, and perhaps the change is documented. Information about the breach, its cause, its remedy, as well as information about precautions and the potential for recurrence, is rarely communicated to anyone outside of IT. Policies or standards may or may not be updated to reflect the new system configuration.

An experience-based program relies on personnel—managers, IT or system administrators, or other persons immediately involved in the situation—to understand and resolve the issue and test the result. The confirmation effort is carried out thoroughly; the system is repaired, the organization has resumed full operations, and the illusion of security is reinstated. Little, if anything, however, is documented. Furthermore, not much thought is given to what might happen if the same or a similar situation occurs when that person or department is unavailable.

A documented program has all the paperwork completed, the policies in place, and the systems and components inventoried. However, when an event occurs, the entire system comes under suspicion because little, if anything, has been tested. No one knows if the system is configured according to policy, if everything is working properly, or indeed, working at all. When no one knows what is working, it's difficult to discover what isn't working.

The technology, organization, and processes of a formal program are both *documented* and *confirmed*. Policies and procedures are not only in place, but executive management is assured that everyone in the organization has been informed of them and, if required, tested. The components and systems have been confirmed; flaws and vulnerabilities have been identified, catalogued, remediated, and reconfirmed. When an event occurs, the organization slips into crisis mode, but does not succumb to chaos. The roles have been defined, the processes are understood, and the actions are initiated.

> Thirteen percent of respondents have integrated business continuity and disaster recovery plans that address recovering the entire enterprise. Seven percent indicated they have no documented plans in place.

Digital security means more than securing servers and keeping out hackers. It means ensuring the organization's digital assets are secure at every step of the business cycle and at every point in time, to the degree that can be achieved. It means ensuring that executive management is not just informed of but actively involved in the creation, implementation, and maintenance of digital security systems by streamlining the channels of communication between management and security teams. Highly effective digital security can only be realized by an organization when business and security objectives are aligned, when the focus on security is proactive in its approach and enterprise-wide in scope, and when the digital security program includes formal processes to ensure that all aspects of it are continuously maintained, updated, and validated.

Companies that operate far from the digital frontier because they have low usage of and reliance on digital technology face a proportionately low probability of a security event and a correspondingly low risk of impact from such an occurrence. As depicted in Figure 2.7, if an

FIGURE 2.7   Technology Drives the Requirements for a World-Class Digital
Security Program

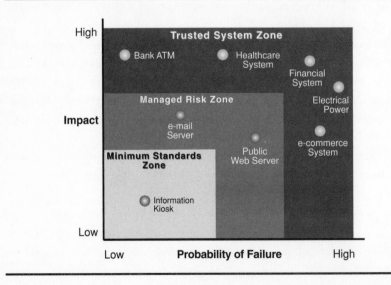

organization has an informational web site that is not connected to internal information systems, there is probably little reliance on the site for anything other than public relations. If it is hacked or defaced, it can be taken offline and recovered without the event inflicting significant damage to the company. However, as also shown in Figure 2.7, as an organization that deploys an e-commerce system increases its usage and reliance on digital technology and moves along the trajectory toward the digital frontier, the probability of a security event occurring increases as does the impact the damage of that event could inflict. This situation drives stricter security requirements and, as Figure 2.8 shows, to meet those requirements, the digital security program has to exhibit the six characteristics to effectively manage risk. It must be a trusted system.

As the company has increased its usage and reliance on technology, that stand-alone web site has become an interactive tool used by customers and clients to place or check on orders, or to review private information. Although these enhancements increase productivity and

FIGURE 2.8   Foundation of a World-Class Digital Security Program

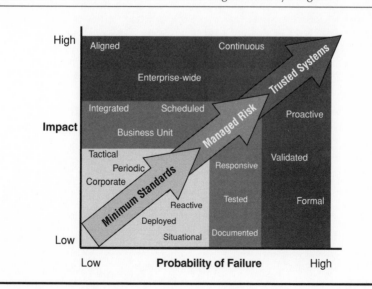

performance, they also increase the organization's risk of facing a serious security incident. Therefore, the company has an increased need for security in terms of both scope and expertise. Reactive digital security must move to a proactive state. Periodic digital security must move to a continuous state. Each characteristic must improve over time. In essence, the organization has to move from applying minimal security standards to developing trusted systems. Before the company moved toward the frontier, it might not have had a pressing need to have a highly effective digital security program in place. It now does. Technology that increases productivity also increases risk. That risk can be addressed and mitigated by a digital security program that exhibits these six characteristics.

When an organization's executive management has the ability to define these characteristics within the parameters of the organization and communicate the importance of these characteristics to the organization, then the executive management will enable the organization to meet the challenge of the digital frontier by executing a digital security agenda.

3

Organizational Components and Security Objectives

Throughout Part One of this book, we've identified the challenge of digital security and mapped out the digital frontier and the digital security frontier. We've described some of the more significant threats and vulnerabilities and established the attributes of a world-class digital security program. This chapter addresses the third challenge facing organizations at the edge of the digital frontier: What will drive an organization to design and implement an aligned, enterprise-wide, continuous, proactive, validated, and formal digital security program? What is the structure of such a program? What are its building blocks? Its parameters?

The guiding principle in devising a digital security program is the same one that drives construction of any kind: The structure must be stable. With regard to digital security, a stable program is one that can be described as effective, maintained, and balanced. It must be balanced with regard to its expertise and leadership at both the technical and managerial levels. There must be balance in the flow of communication between those levels, especially with regard to situations in which the business objectives and security objectives may not be completely integrated or understood. Executive management must strive to achieve balance between desired results and available resources; the digital security team must strive to achieve balance between productivity and asset protection.

FIGURE 3.1   Organizational Components Support the Six Characteristics of a
World-Class Digital Security Program

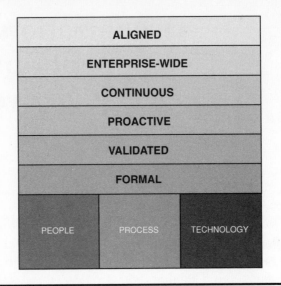

The reason that stability is so important to a security structure is that
a properly balanced program will be able to adapt as the environment
changes, and the digital security environment changes frequently and
rapidly. It isn't just the threats that change; the building blocks of a security program are dynamic. These building blocks are the people, process,
and technology that comprise the organization and make it work. As the
program evolves to meet new challenges, the parameters will change as
well because they are determined by the value the organization assigns
to those building blocks (see Figure 3.1).

ORGANIZATIONAL COMPONENTS

The success of a highly effective digital security program depends on
the value placed on the most important assets a business possesses: its
people, its process, and its technology (PPT). When these three elements

work together in a fluid, responsive, continually changing environment, they generate results that form the core of the program and provide its greatest strength (Figure 3.2).

People

People refers to how a digital security organization is structured, what roles and responsibilities are assigned, and what skills and knowledge are present. The people component contains the critical success factor for a digital security program: *adaptability.* An organization can deploy the best digital security technology available, but if the people component is weak, the digital security program will fail to meet its objectives. For example, if a software application monitored systems 24 hours a day and sent warnings to the security staff alerting them to unauthorized attempts to gain access to the network, that software would be helpful. However, if not enough people were available to receive and respond to the warnings in a timely fashion, or they were not trained in proper response countermeasures, it is likely that the return on the investment from digital security tools would not be fully realized.

FIGURE 3.2   Organizational Components

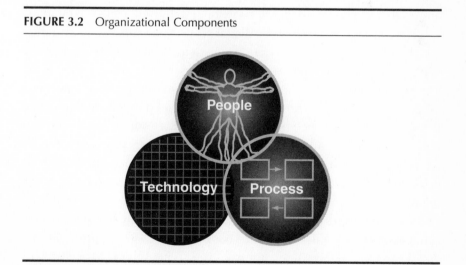

Highly effective digital security programs invest in the people component of the program. A formal, hierarchical but empowered structure must be established that clearly outlines authority and accountability and enables personnel to focus on securing the organization's digital assets. Staffing must be adequate to fulfill the stated security objectives, and clear roles and responsibilities must be defined, documented, and understood. The staff must be experienced with regard to security, technology, business, and communication issues, and trained with regard to potential scenarios. These skills must be fostered and continually developed to ensure the program maintains pace with technological and organization requirements and can adapt quickly to situations as they arise.

Process

The *process* component of a digital security program refers to the approved approaches or activities to be followed when executing all phases and aspects of the program. These approaches or activities can range from determining how digital security policies are approved, to how and when all personnel are trained in security-related issues, to the steps to follow when a web site is hacked or a system infiltrated. Having formal processes in place provides many benefits, but the key benefit is to ensure that all actions taken will be within established policy boundaries.

The process component for digital security is similar to its counterpart in a business unit. For example, expenses incurred by employees while conducting business may be reimbursable if certain policies and procedures have been followed, and in most cases, the reimbursement process is uneventful. The process was established to ensure that policy is followed, and that specific information, in this example, expenses, can be processed in an efficient manner. If a digital security program is to operate consistently and effectively, repeatable procedures must be documented, understood, and *executed*. This includes procedures for initiating and implementing changes to existing policies and processes.

An established process for approving changes to security policies can mean the difference between a consistent, four-week approval cycle and a four-to-sixteen-week approval cycle. This time lag translates to having a digital security program that can respond to a changing environment within a reasonable amount of time, or one that cannot. Likewise, during an intrusion incident, having an established response procedure can mean the difference between losing customer information stored on one server, and losing customer information stored on 10 servers. Having an established response procedure can mean the difference between minimizing the impact of an intrusion event, and being unable to determine exactly which assets have been compromised.

Some organizations go a step beyond security training to implementing programs to validate policy compliance. Although the government most commonly employs this process, commercial entities are rapidly recognizing the value of certification programs. For example, if policies exist that require personnel in specific roles to have specific, predefined requirements or certifications, certain development or training efforts can be streamlined or eliminated while ensuring that systems are consistently developed and implemented according to accepted standards. The degree to which organizations develop and implement security policy is clearly an executive management decision that must be based on the aligned business and security objectives. Although recognized industry standards are a good benchmark, they do not meet the needs of organizations universally. It will take time for organizations to develop, implement, and maintain a policy infrastructure that clearly supports their risk model, and the accompanying technological infrastructure.

Technology

Bad people and bad process cannot be fixed with technology. In fact, technology can take a bad process and make bad things happen faster or can drive away untrained people. Expertly deployed technology, coupled with trained, security-minded people and processes that are understood and followed, can enable an organization to realize significant productivity gains.

The *technology* component of a digital security program includes specialized software or tools focused on digital security, such as firewalls, public key infrastructure (PKI), user ID management, and an intrusion detection system (IDS). However, it also includes the planning for and configuration of other, platform-specific software or systems, such as Unix operating systems, hand-held mobile computers, and various types of routers. The technology components of digital security can include any hardware, software, or device used to store or process digital assets or intellectual capital.

Like other technology components, digital security technology is commonly deployed to increase overall productivity. Furthermore, as with deploying and operating other technology components, adequate planning and design must take place to ensure a return will be realized on the investment. Those returns could include increasing or exceeding required service levels, reducing the effort to achieve required service levels, or simply enabling the digital security program to meet required service levels.

Today's globally interconnected world affords tremendous opportunities to share information; however, it also abounds with an ever-increasing number of threats to the integrity of organizational infrastructures. This situation presents tremendous technical challenges with regard to increasing productivity while protecting digital assets. An executive officer understands that elements of each of the solution components—the people, the process, and the technology—must change to make an appreciable difference in the security climate of an organization. If the people, the process, and the technology remain unchanged, there will be no improvement. The executive management of organizations striving to implement a digital security program must understand technology and know how to leverage it in order to achieve aligned business and security objectives.

SECURITY OBJECTIVES

Building the six characteristics of a highly effective digital security program into the framework of an organization's digital security structure requires an understanding of the fundamental tenets of digital security in technical terms as well as in terms of their application. As we have stated elsewhere, business objectives and security objectives must be aligned, and the goals of performance and productivity must be balanced according to those objectives. These concepts go to the heart of applied digital security: what the organization's digital security program must accomplish, and how it can go about doing that without undue interference in the core business agenda.

Confidentiality, Integrity, and Availability

Confidentiality, integrity, and availability (CIA) are the most basic premises of information protection and therefore, are the central tenets of any digital security program. *Confidentiality* assumes that data in its many states, including data in transit and data at rest, is protected from compromise, including unauthorized access or disclosure. This includes the protection of data to ensure that it does not exist; that is, when it has been deleted, it has been completely deleted. For example, when data is moved from a repository—a database, network, or even a hard drive— there must be safeguards in place to ensure that the reassignment or reclassification of that database, network, or hard drive will not subject digital information assets to compromise. Closely aligned with the concept of confidentiality, *integrity* assumes that data, in transit or at rest and in any repository, is protected from unauthorized modification or deletion. *Availability* provides the counterbalancing assumption that data is and will remain accessible on demand by authorized users.

Although these objectives are central to the foundation of any digital security program, they are only objectives and require tools in order to be achieved. The fundamental discipline in the attempt to achieve CIA is to control access to digital assets. This discipline is called access control.

Access Control

Any security system must have in place the proper tools to issue permissions, grant entry, and verify identities in order for it to function effectively. In the realm of digital security, however, it is critical to have such mechanisms in place. Determining the parameters of those mechanisms depends largely on the values held by the organization and the value it places on its digital assets, but the basic functions of the mechanisms are fixed. Achieving the optimum level of security requires that the system must know who is allowed to enter and where they are allowed to go; it must verify that the person using the system is indeed the authorized user; and it must perform these functions at every log-on and access attempt. The core methods used to control access are called *authentication* and *authorization*; management of these methods is referred to as *administration*. These elements have a solid footing in the IT world as "the three As." We consider a fourth, less frequently discussed "A" to be just as important to deploying effective digital security: *auditing*. These four elements are discussed below.

Authorization procedures involve assigning permissions to access specific digital assets. Common permissions include read or write access. Such permissions may be based on hierarchy, need-to-know or project-related status, or any number of organization-specific requirements.

Authentication procedures involve establishing identity, and many security practitioners view authentication as the first line of defense for information systems. It is commonly held that users are authenticated through three factors: *knowledge* (something that you *know*, i.e., a password), *possession* (something that you *have,* i.e., random password generator or smartcard), and *identification* (something that you *are*, i.e., fingerprints or retinal scan).

From a business perspective, authentication is arguably the most important of the three access control tools. If an organization's digital assets are to be truly secured, the security system must know who is in the system with a reasonable to high degree of certainty prior to that person gaining access to any nonpublic information. Knowing who is in the system facilitates tracking users' movements to determine where they are and what they are doing. Ultimately, the goal for access control schemes is to establish accountability; that is, for every action on a system, that action can be traced back to a single user. For example, if an authorized user attempts to gain access to a system or asset prohibited to him or her, it could constitute a threat or it could be an innocent mistake. Either way, management has a means of knowing who attempted access. However, if authentication procedures are lax, or group authentications are allowed, management's ability to assess the action is limited; should the action be the precursor to an intrusion or an attack, there is little accountability and therefore little recourse.

Administration involves the management of authentication credentials and authorization privileges. Effective administration can help resolve some key issues in digital security. One issue is the failure to revoke user privileges within a timely manner when employees separate from the organization or transfer within the organization to different positions or projects that have different security profiles. In both cases, the employees or ex-employees retain authorized access to systems they should not be able to enter. Although authentication, authorization, and administration are critical to attaining and maintaining access control, a digital security program cannot be described as highly effective if no one is monitoring or auditing the system for failed authentication attempts or for authorized users attempting unauthorized activities.

The *auditing* activities undertaken by the digital security program should not be confused with activities undertaken during a financial audit. Auditing from a digital security program perspective involves activities to assess the effectiveness of the people, process, and technology that make up the digital security program. Assessments are conducted to ensure that policy, procedures, and standards are implemented and followed, testing the real effectiveness of the digital security program. The view that auditing is the "fourth A" of access control may not be widely held in the industry; therefore auditing is often addressed with less diligence or relegated to a lower priority than the other elements of access control. However, auditing helps ensure that authentication and authorization controls remain in effect and, for that reason, we consider it fundamental.

Systematically monitoring and reviewing system logs is the only way that system administrators will know who is in the system at any given time and what they are doing or trying to do; it is also the only way they will know when intruders are trying to gain access or if employees are trying to gain access to information they are not authorized to see. Mistakes in security configuration settings or an undiscovered vulnerability can leave a system exposed to unauthorized access.

Audit procedures involve continual evaluation of the output of various access control systems in search of unauthorized activities. When discovered, these unauthorized activities can be reported to management and the appropriate responses can be initiated. It is important to note that digital security auditing is not an activity that can be performed periodically; it requires continuous effort to achieve effective returns.

The framework for a highly effective digital security program includes the components, organizational models, and objectives that populate its structure. When considered together, these fundamental elements form the foundation of a practical program that will enable an organization to restrict access to digital assets appropriately, to run the program effectively and achieve security objectives, and to recover when security events occur.

Part Two of this book provides in-depth consideration of specific items that an organization must use to construct the environment of a digital security program. By building on the framework suggested, this material provides constructive guidance on real-world security issues and provides end-state solutions that will help accomplish the objective of defending the digital frontier by instituting a digital security program.

PART TWO
The Agenda for Action

While always exhilarating, life at the frontier has never been easy. Regardless of the era or their place in history, pioneers are never complacent. By definition, life on any frontier is fraught with uncertainties and dangers, but it holds an allure the adventurous find difficult to ignore. Pioneers at the edge of nineteenth-century America's western frontier faced a daunting prospect. What lay before them held the potential for untold riches and success; it also held an equal potential for disaster. Business organizations at the edge of the digital frontier face a similar situation, and their executive management must exhibit the same strength of purpose, the same will to succeed, the same determination to carve out a stake, lay claim to it, and then defend it with vigor and diligence, as did the pioneers.

The world faced by America's frontiersmen was unimaginably vast, foreign, harsh, and hostile in parts. It held challenges they could plan for, such as the probable duration of the journey, the terrain, wildlife, and known weather patterns. But it also held challenges they could not predict: weather anomalies, breakdowns, detours, illnesses, and local political unrest. Still they went, in numbers that bear out the irresistible urge to tame what hadn't been tamed before.

Some threats to a twenty-first century organization's digital security, such as viruses, can be expected. When they strike is not so much the issue as knowing they will eventually, and being prepared to respond quickly and appropriately when they do. Such threats occur with enough frequency worldwide that organizations with digital security programs in place should be able to deflect or thwart them without reaching the crisis stage. However, latent threats and vulnerabilities exist as well and, like the pioneers' unknowns, these threats are more difficult to prepare to face. These threats may come in the form of malignant code that has not yet been triggered, or invasive technology currently under development, or any number of occurrences of catastrophic proportions that defy imagination. Organizations at the digital frontier must have measures in place that will enable them to handle the unforeseen, the unpredictable, and even the unimaginable with the same reasoned response given to a routine hacking episode.

Part Two of this book provides organizations with a framework to achieve such a level of digital security by designing a program according to a three-part security agenda: Restrict, Run, and Recover[SM].[1] This security agenda presents an enterprise view of risk-mitigating items; provides a framework for discussion, action, and measurement of issues and responses; and outlines a digital security posture that relies on the interaction of people, process, and technology to provide a world-class defense of organizational digital assets. The security agenda includes the nine dimensions of an on-going cycle of asset protection:

1. Having the ability to detect intrusions and viruses.
2. Having effective incident response programs in place.
3. Enacting privacy measures that will allow the appropriate degrees of both transparency and protection.

4. Defining and disseminating comprehensive policies, standards, and guidelines related to data and data protection.
5. Enhancing the physical security of components and infrastructure.
6. Implementing asset and service management strategies.
7. Determining and managing exploitable vulnerabilities.
8. Managing user access.
9. Ensuring business continuity during a crisis.

When an organization facing the challenges of the digital frontier understands the importance of applying the key security characteristics outlined in Chapter 2 to the organization's people, process, and technology, as described in Chapter 3, it will have set the foundation of its digital defense posture. The security agenda outlined in Chapters 4 and 5 presents the plan for building the superstructure that will support that posture.

4

The Security Agenda

A ny comprehensive digital security program must satisfy three
critical mandates:

1. It must enable the organization to protect and monitor access to
   systems and data.
2. It must enable the organization to operate at the highest level of
   productivity while enhancing performance to the degree possible.
3. It must enable the organization to sustain an attack, absorb the
   impact, and regain full functionality, and do so within a time-
   sensitive context.

RESTRICT, RUN, AND RECOVER^{SM}

The security agenda has streamlined these wide-ranging operational
aspects of a well-designed digital security program into three major
components: Restrict, Run, and Recover^{SM}, known as "the three Rs" of
digital security. When a digital security program includes measures
that address all three components of the security agenda, the organization has initiated control and containment capabilities that lead to risk

---

FIGURE 4.1 The Security Agenda

Policies, Standards, & Guidelines

Intrusion & Virus Detection

Incident Response

Physical Security

Privacy

Asset & Service Management

Vulnerability Management

Entitlement Management

Business Continuity

---

reduction and management. As shown in Figure 4.1, this three-part security agenda comprises nine specific items that enable an organization to achieve a high level of digital security. Subsequent sections describe the capabilities for executing those items to full deployment.

The foundation of a highly effective digital security program is to ensure the confidentiality, integrity, and availability of digital assets by restricting the accessibility of those assets to persons who have an established need for access to them and prohibiting access by others. The *principle of least privilege* guides this effort because restricting access appropriately is a balancing act. If access is limited too severely, functionality is compromised; if access is not controlled tightly enough, security is compromised. To enable an organization to identify and maintain this balance in restricting access to digital assets, there must be a focus on the five items that combine to form the *Restrict* agenda.

The next component of the security agenda, the *Run* agenda, supports data integrity and authorized access to data, which enable organizations to gain efficient access to information and to automate and realize efficiencies with respect to managing digital entitlements, vulnerabilities, assets, and services. The final component of the security agenda, the *Recover* agenda, addresses the issue of having organizationally appropriate plans in place to ensure a full recovery from negative impacts. It does so by creating an environment that supports the secure retention and recoverability of critical digital assets, and by identifying the components of people and processes that must be in place to ensure availability and continuity.

SECURITY AGENDA ITEMS

Building a digital security program based on the nine dimensions of digital security that comprise the security agenda enables an organization to move from a position of having an inconsistent or unbalanced security posture to attaining world-class status. Earlier, we defined the characteristics that describe a highly effective digital security program: aligned, enterprise-wide, continuous, proactive, validated, and formal. These six characteristics represent the "whats" of digital security: what the program should look like, what elements of the organization it should encompass, and what the program should do for the organization. The nine agenda items are the "hows" of digital security. They provide a clear picture of each significant area of risk and the program element that should be put in place to mitigate or eliminate that risk. The agenda items show members of the executive management team how to look for vulnerabilities, how to determine the organization's degree of risk, and how to address those issues. The agenda items work together to form the core of the digital security program by providing a technical architecture and internal controls that enable an organization to achieve highly effective digital security.

The agenda items are grouped by their utilities within the parameters of the digital security program. The first agenda item within the designation Restrict is intrusion and virus detection. This system alerts network and systems administrators and the digital security team when unauthorized persons have gained access to systems or networks, or when unauthorized activity is taking place. Incident response provides the initial response to an incident and continues to address the ramifications of the event through to resolution while working with the intrusion and virus detection group to contain the damage and control its effects. Privacy enables a comprehensive approach to achieving and maintaining compliance with all internal or industry privacy-related directives as well as federal or state regulations. The policies, standards, and guidelines agenda item provides a structure for a comprehensive education and documentation effort that can be disseminated throughout the organization to ensure complete awareness and understanding of digital security concerns and their importance. The physical security agenda item provides a framework for merging traditional security programs with digital security concerns to provide a total digital security program that will protect digital assets and the infrastructure that supports their use.

When the Restrict agenda items have been substantially deployed, the Run agenda items serve to support and maintain their implementation. The Run agenda items include asset and service management, which provides an integrated system to effectively manage and track assets and support services while increasing accountability and productivity. Vulnerability management provides centralized, automated tracking, monitoring, and mitigation of exploitable weaknesses at the system, platform, and application levels. Entitlement management enables organizations to implement, manage, and enforce access control measures to safeguard systems.

The Recover agenda contains only one item, which addresses what may well be the most critical issue an organization can face: business continuity. Preventive measures are unquestionably important to have in place; however, if a digital attack of sufficient magnitude occurs and overwhelms those mechanisms, the organization may sustain heavy, even catastrophic damage. It is unlikely that an efficient, effective recovery will ensue if the organization does not have a plan in place to direct recovery and continuity efforts. The business continuity agenda item provides a framework for organizations to create executable plans that will ensure the recovery of mission-critical data, processes, and systems, and the continuation of business operations.

A company that has addressed and implemented these nine agenda items still cannot be considered secure until it is assured that each of

FIGURE 4.2 World-Class Digital Security[1]

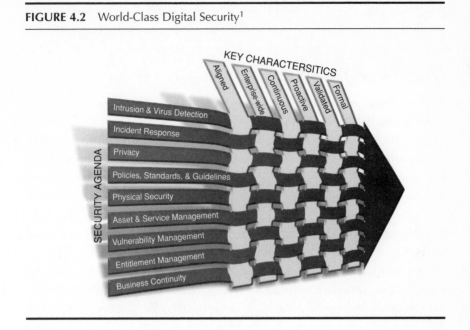

the nine items has been fully deployed and can be described as having the six characteristics outlined in Chapter 2. As shown in Figure 4.2, each agenda item must be deployed in such a way that the security objectives of each item could be described as aligned, enterprise-wide, continuous, proactive, validated, and formal. When the agenda items have been fully deployed and exhibit the six characteristics, as shown in Figure 4.2, digital security has been woven into the fabric of the organization.

PLANNING, ARCHITECTURE, OPERATIONS, AND MONITORING CAPABILITIES

After the digital security needs of an organization have been determined, and the parameters of the nine agenda items have been defined by the organization, deploying those agenda items becomes the priority. To effectively deploy the agenda items, an organization must be capable of planning, designing, operating, and monitoring a digital security program. This section details these capabilities and their execution, and presents a comprehensive matrix showing them for each agenda item.

Organizational Model

The organizational structure of the digital security program includes linkages to other functions not under direct control of the security officer, for example, public, media, and government relations; physical security; privacy; and business continuity. The Chief Information Security Officer (CISO) is central to the success of the digital security program. In placing the CISO, the CEO delegates the authority, responsibility, and accountability to manage risk to digital assets in the organization. In this capacity, the CISO must have access to and receive input from those at the highest levels of executive management.

In an ideal situation, as shown in the top half of Figure 4.3, the CISO would report directly to an officer in the company, although this is only likely to happen in a large organization, for instance a *Fortune* 500 firm. In smaller organizations, it is more common for the CISO to report to a manager or director two or three levels below the CEO, and even then, the reporting configuration usually remains within the purview of the IT organization.

Attempting to make strategic decisions that address managing risk while reporting within the IT organization presents additional challenges. For instance, it is possible that the Chief Information Officer (CIO) and CISO might have conflicting primary goals. While both officers would agree that confidentiality, integrity, and availability are critical security objectives, the primary goal of the CISO is to protect the confidentiality and integrity of information and the primary goal of the CIO is availability of information. The distinction is based on their respective positions within the organizations, and such a situation suggests that the most effective hierarchical structure would be peer status for these roles.

Bearing strategic responsibilities to manage risk, the CISO position is clearly executive-level and therefore requires significant business and communication skills. The CISO serves as an advisor to other executive managers to facilitate deployment of the technology required to achieve

FIGURE 4.3   Digital Security Model
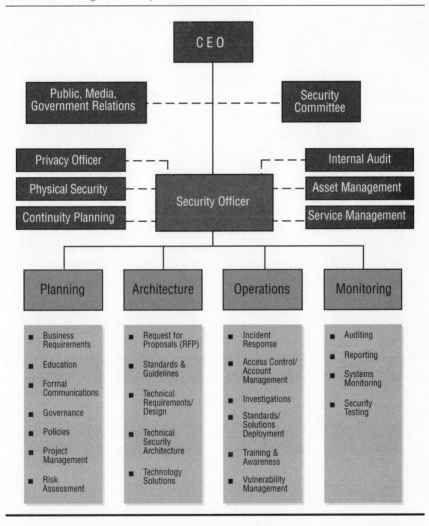

productivity gains while minimizing the risk associated with increased reliance upon that technology. The CISO directs the organization's efforts to acquire capabilities to run a highly effective digital security program and ensure that the program can provide for the changing requirements of the organization and its shareholders, employees, and customers.

Capabilities

As shown in the lower half of Figure 4.3, the model of a highly effective digital security program includes the development of four distinct yet integrated capabilities: planning, architecture, operations, and monitoring (PAOM). Each of these four capabilities plays a vital role within each agenda item. This set of security capabilities provides an enterprise-wide structural framework that enables execution of the nine security agenda items. This framework can assist the digital security architects as they deploy technology to meet the organization's digital security objectives. Once implemented, the PAOM framework can be used as a model for measuring the success of a digital security program or segments of it. All of the agenda items discussed within the context of PAOM are interconnected but can function independent of each other as the organization moves toward the goal of a fully optimized, digital security program.

It is through the framework established by the PAOM capabilities that digital security is implemented into an organization. The digital security *planning* team has responsibility for tasks such as formalizing the organization's IT governance model, conducting risk assessments, directing security education efforts, managing the formal documentation effort, and providing project management on digital security-related projects. The *architecture* team bears responsibility for developing security configuration standards, analyzing and developing potential digital security technical solutions, and designing the overall architecture for the digital security program. The *operations* team holds responsibility for the day-to-day implementation and smooth functionality of systems, applications, and networks. These responsibilities include granting and revoking user privileges, vulnerability and account management, technical security configuration deployment, ensuring security awareness, and responding appropriately to potential issues. The primary focus of the *monitoring* team is to observe and audit systems, examine them for anomalies, and to report on compliance with policies.

It is important to note that the policies, standards, and guidelines agenda item's initial value to an organization is that it grants the digital security team the authority to run the digital security program and present to the entire enterprise the executive-sponsored direction for digital security. This direction is presented via formally documented policies that establish technical configuration settings for specific technologies according to industry or in-house standards and that provide direction for managing digital security throughout the enterprise by implementing guidelines. The core policy set should include policies that describe the function of the digital security program, state the importance of and management support for digital security, outline a security committee that provides oversight to the program, establish roles and responsibilities with respect to digital security, identify laws and regulations requiring compliance, and outline a framework for digital asset classification, asset management, change management, and waiver management. Figure 4.4 presents all the aspects of the PAOM capabilities. Figure 4.5 presents all aspects within the PAOM capabilities as they relate to each digital security agenda item.

Planning

The planning capability of a digital security program is the cornerstone of formalization of the program. All capabilities and agenda items should have their roots in planning, whether in the initial creation and deployment of the capability or agenda item or in their ongoing maintenance and care. Planning for digital security helps ensure that the program delivers the level of security that is required by the organization. Planning accomplishes this in part by ensuring that ad hoc approaches

FIGURE 4.4 Aspects of the PAOM Capabilities

Planning	Architecture	Operations	Monitoring
▪ Business Requirements ▪ Education ▪ Formal Communications ▪ Governance ▪ Policies ▪ Project Management ▪ Risk Assessment	▪ Requests for Proposals (RFP) ▪ Standards & Guidelines ▪ Technical Requirements/Design ▪ Technical Security Architecture ▪ Technology Solutions	▪ Incident Response ▪ Access Control/Account Management ▪ Investigations ▪ Standards/Solutions Deployment ▪ Training & Awareness ▪ Vulnerability Management	▪ Auditing ▪ Reporting ▪ Systems Monitoring ▪ Security Testing

FIGURE 4.5   Aspects of the PAOM Capabilities Broken Out by Agenda Item

Agenda Item	Planning	Architecture	Operations	Monitoring
Restrict				
Intrusion & Virus Detection	▪ Policies ▪ Business Requirements ▪ Project Management ▪ Education ▪ Formal Communications	▪ Standards & Guidelines ▪ RFP ▪ Technical Requirements/Design ▪ Technology Solutions	▪ Solutions Deployment ▪ Vulnerability Management ▪ Incident Response	▪ Systems Monitoring ▪ Security Testing ▪ Reporting
Incident Response	▪ Policies ▪ Business Requirements ▪ Project Management ▪ Education ▪ Formal Communications	▪ Standards & Guidelines ▪ RFP ▪ Technology Solutions	▪ Standards/Solutions Deployment ▪ Training & Awareness ▪ Incident Response ▪ Investigations	▪ Reporting ▪ Auditing
Privacy	▪ Policies ▪ Risk Assessment ▪ Governance ▪ Business Requirements ▪ Formal Communications	▪ Standards & Guidelines ▪ Formal Communications ▪ Technical Requirements/Design ▪ Technical Security Architecture ▪ Technology Solutions	▪ Standards/Solutions Deployment ▪ Training & Awareness ▪ Vulnerability Management ▪ Access Control/Account Management ▪ Investigations ▪ Incident Response	▪ Auditing ▪ Systems Monitoring
Policies, Standards, & Guidelines	▪ Policies ▪ Formal Communications ▪ Governance	▪ Standards & Guidelines ▪ Technology Solutions	▪ Standards Deployment ▪ Training & Awareness ▪ Vulnerability Management	▪ Auditing
Physical	▪ Policies ▪ Formal Communications ▪ Risk Assessment ▪ Governance	▪ Standards & Guidelines	▪ Standards Deployment ▪ Investigations ▪ Training & Awareness ▪ Access Control/Account Management	▪ Auditing
Run				
Entitlement Management	▪ Policies ▪ Risk Assessment ▪ Education ▪ Project Management ▪ Business Requirements ▪ Formal Communications	▪ Standards & Guidelines ▪ Technical Requirements/Design ▪ Technical Security Architecture ▪ Technology Solutions	▪ Standards/Solutions Deployment ▪ Training & Awareness ▪ Access Control/Account Management	▪ Auditing ▪ Systems Monitoring
Asset & Service Management	▪ Policies ▪ Formal Communications ▪ Risk Assessment ▪ Education ▪ Project Management ▪ Business Requirements	▪ Standards & Guidelines ▪ Technical Requirements/Design ▪ Technical Security Architecture ▪ Technology Solutions	▪ Standards/Solutions Deployment ▪ Training & Awareness ▪ Vulnerability Management ▪ Access Control/Account Management	▪ Auditing ▪ Systems Monitoring
Vulnerability Management	▪ Policies ▪ Formal Communications ▪ Risk Assessment ▪ Education ▪ Project Management ▪ Business Requirements	▪ Standards & Guidelines ▪ Technical Requirements/Design ▪ Technical Security Architecture ▪ Technology Solutions	▪ Standards/Solutions Deployment ▪ Training & Awareness ▪ Vulnerability Management	▪ Auditing ▪ Systems Monitoring
Recover				
Business Continuity	▪ Risk Assessment ▪ Governance ▪ Education ▪ Project Management ▪ Formal Communications ▪ Business Requirements	▪ Standards & Guidelines ▪ Technical Requirements/Design ▪ Technical Security Architecture ▪ Technology Solutions ▪ RFP	▪ Standards/Solutions Deployment ▪ Training & Awareness	▪ Auditing

to capabilities and agenda items are minimized and eliminated, that all efforts are driven by business requirements, and that efforts are targeted where the most risk exists.

When these capabilities are in place and operational, the digital security program has begun to take on two characteristics of a highly effective program: aligned and formal. It has become aligned in the sense that executive management is now directing digital security considerations instead of delegating them. The program has become formal in the sense that management-approved policies have been documented, communicated to every member of the organization, and followed by executing the digital security program functions. Once a formal digital security program has been established, the digital security team's focus can shift toward improving and implementing additional security services that involve establishment of additional goals, assignment of resources, and development of procedures.

Aspects of Planning

Business Requirements   Business requirements establish the need for capabilities, aspects, and items that make up the digital security program. Each capability and item exist to support one or more business requirement. Requirements function as the measuring stick for capabilities, aspects, and items. If the capabilities and items are meeting the business requirements for risk mitigation, digital security objectives are being met; if not, the organization must take action to improve the capability, item, or aspect of the digital security program.

Education   The objective of security education is to develop and maintain the skill sets of the enterprise security organization. Whereas a security awareness program focuses on end users and topics that address operational systems, an education program addresses the technical skills of the organization as needed to ensure that knowledge of leading practices, industry or regulatory issues, and new technologies is maintained.

Policy   This aspect of planning encompasses two fundamental functions: the development and maintenance of security policies that give direction to standards and guidelines, and the development of a waiver framework to manage deviations from policies, standards, and guidelines. Performing these functions ensures that the security policies, standards, and guidelines are kept up to date, are enforced, and have variances documented as necessary in formal waivers.

Formal Communications This aspect of planning encompasses several fundamental functions not addressed by the digital security policies, specifically the development of procedures for achieving goals and measuring goal attainment within the program. The process of measuring performance against goals can be reported to the appropriate parties in scorecards. A scorecard is a vehicle to communicate status and performance against goals. This ensures that progress is sustainable and predictable as the organization moves toward the goal of having a world-class digital security program. This aspect of planning is also responsible for reporting the status of digital security items and capabilities to the CEO, the security committee, management, and employees. A common communications structure (scorecards) and procedures are determined and followed when communicating to the organization. Scorecard information is approved by the CISO prior to distribution. Digital security information is provided to the planning, architecture, operations, and monitoring teams.

Governance Governance is the process of ensuring that controls are adequately applied throughout the enterprise to reduce risk. This oversight also ensures that management stays informed of current risks and that there is a formal mechanism to communicate both objectives and risks within the digital security program as the organization changes.

Project Management Project management within the digital security program includes the development of the overall program budget, developing plans for the assessment and implementation of new elements of the security architecture, vendor selection, and contract management for software, systems, and services. Project management is also provided for implementing and improving capabilities and agenda items.

Risk Assessment This includes defining the scope of analysis, identifying environments and assets for review, evaluating the importance of assets within company operations, identifying threats to assets, vulnerabilities, and compensating controls, developing a risk profile for the assessed environment, and developing a risk reduction plan for the environment.

Architecture

The architecture processes in a digital security program involve the translation of security policies and objectives into technical requirements, standards, and solution designs. The architecture team establishes a model that defines the integration between technologies, business processes, and policy. One key function in architecture is the development of a formal method or repeatable process of integrating security controls into the design of digital information systems. Architecture functions also include technical research and development of technologies that support the evolution of the system architecture.

Aspects of Architecture

Request for Information/Request for Proposal (RFI/RFP) Development
This entails ensuring that RFI/RFPs include adequate digital security requirements or documentation, and working with RFI/RFP recipients to clarify details to ensure that digital security is considered as the organization acquires new technologies.

Technical Requirements Design An architecture team must be able to describe and map a piece or pieces of technology to the fulfillment of a business requirement.

Technical Security Architecture This aspect of digital security architecture incorporates the design and structure of the security components that support an organization's ability to defend its digital frontier. It includes the communication of this technical security architecture to the organization as a part of the overall security services provided to the organization.

Technology Solutions This aspect entails researching and developing new technology solutions for the enterprise, enabling the enterprise to deploy security measures concurrent with the deployment of new applications or infrastructure. The technology solutions function is a formal liaison between the digital security team and the IT department, and provides the enterprise with a mechanism for technical assessment of design alternatives if waivers to policy and standards are required. This aspect is also responsible for assessing waivers that document situations in which a digital asset operates outside of compliance with digital security policy. The assessment of waivers includes identifying options and creating a road map for bringing the digital asset into compliance with policy.

Operations

Digital security operations are those tasks or processes in the security program that are generally performed on a day-to-day basis to provide security services to the organization. Since these functions are numerous, they have a strong tendency to be distributed throughout the enterprise. When assessing, designing, or implementing the digital security operations function, the objective is to create the most efficient process that supports appropriate segregation of duties and supports the availability of digital assets. Security operations models can be distributed or consolidated and, in ideal cases, many of these tasks are automated.

Aspects of Operations

Incident Response   This aspect of the operations function is responsible for responding to verified digital security incidents in such a manner as to minimize impact to the organization. This is accomplished by bringing together cross-functional teams with skills that are pertinent to each individual incident.

Access Control/Account Management   This entails coordinating, creating, and maintaining effective controls for user account management and access controls for all user IDs and access profiles within the enterprise. This may also include the management of third-party access to applications in outsourcing situations and management of business-to-consumer, business-to-business, and business-to-employee operations.

Investigations   The formal analysis of digital assets in support of bona fide digital security incidents is a critical step that precedes the exezcution of a formal digital forensic investigation. This includes linkages to all pertinent areas, including human resources, legal, and other management functions.

Standards/Solutions Deployment After it has been defined, designed, and tested, a standard or solution must be deployed into the environment to bring about the targeted returns. Standards/solutions deployment covers the actual implementation of standards or technical solutions into the target environment. Beyond the initial implementation, this also includes deploying periodic updates to existing standards or solutions.

Training and Awareness This aspect of operations includes developing, maintaining, and deploying the security awareness program. The security awareness program should include topics such as password usage, physical security, screen saver usage, virus reporting, and other topics that will ensure the security of the organization's assets. These may include regular communications regarding the organization's security status, and other messages that relay not only the importance of digital security but the awareness that digital security-related events are occurring and being resolved.

Vulnerability Management This aspect involves tracking exploitable weaknesses and maintaining the integrity of information systems by identifying appropriate safeguards and ensuring that potential points of failure are addressed on an enterprise-wide level. This also includes centralized monitoring and automated methods of ensuring that compliance and configurations are maintained throughout the organization.

Monitoring

Monitoring processes in a digital security program ensure that a management mechanism exists to assess the effectiveness of operational processes and that digital security information required for regulatory or other reports is generated as required. When necessary, the monitoring and compliance function assists with response to incidents and helps conduct investigations, in addition to the formal aspects of monitoring.

Aspects of Monitoring

Auditing Auditing includes conducting activities to assess the effectiveness of the people, process, and technology that make up the digital security program. Assessments are conducted to ensure that policy, procedures, and standards are implemented and followed, testing the real effectiveness of the digital security program. Auditing will identify scenarios in which policy, standards, and guidelines are deployed and indicate whether the people, processes, and technologies that deploy them are adequate or are inadequate and require improvement.

Reporting As required by organizational policy or regulation, the digital security program develops required management reports to demonstrate the effectiveness of controls and report any identified lapses.

Systems Monitoring A fully deployed digital security program must be capable of monitoring for unauthorized activity on all digital assets, reviewing various log files for any unauthorized or unrecognized activity, and tracking the state of health of digital security.

Security Testing This function is responsible for executing continuous security tests on all digital assets to ensure digital security countermeasures are working properly.

5

The Three Rs of Digital Security

RESTRICT

The heart of any highly effective digital security program is a solid understanding of what needs to be protected and how the program can provide that protection as efficiently, cost-effectively, and transparently as possible. It is up to the executive management team to empower the digital security team to determine these parameters at the technical level, but just as importantly, executive management must understand what those parameters are and what formalizing them will mean to the organization. Executive management must focus on and sponsor the Restrict items of the security agenda. The Restrict agenda comprises five items that relate to the overall design and functionality of the digital security program itself and thereby establish the criteria for implementing the Run and Recover agendas.

The five Restrict agenda items provide insight into how these items fit into the overall organizational security model, describe specific capabilities required for full deployment and execution of the items, and provide situational devices to underscore their importance to a digital security program. This chapter also describes why it is critical that an organization has in place a strong foundation of clear policies, standards, and guidelines that establish countermeasures, such as intrusion, virus detection, and incident response, and preventive measures, such as privacy and physical security. These preventive measures and counter-measures must not only be in place proactively, they must be under-stood and followed on an enterprise-wide level. The Restrict agenda items focus on determining what the organization needs the digital security program to provide, and what the program needs to protect. The five items within the Restrict agenda are:

1. Intrusion and virus detection, which enables the organization to detect unauthorized access to digital assets.
2. Incident response, which identifies how the organization will respond when a security event occurs.
3. Policies, standards, and guidelines, which enable the organiza-tion to determine and define acceptable behaviors and accept-able risks.
4. Privacy, which addresses the various elements that drive privacy policies, such as laws and regulations, and how they are going to be interpreted and implemented.
5. Physical security, which enables the organization to take a holis-tic approach to security that includes components as well as the environment in which they reside.

Intrusion and Virus Detection

The importance of knowing who is accessing an organization's systems is a fundamental element in a digital security system. Knowing when peo-ple enter and exit a system, where they go and what they do while using a system, and whether they try to do something unusual or prohibited are valuable pieces of information as well, but none of that can be known if users' identities and permissions are not confirmed before they are allowed to access the system.

Knowing that everyone accessing a system is there by invitation or permission is necessary because threats and vulnerabilities can appear with little warning. New software applications, new technologies, and changes to systems all carry inherent threats that can alter the stability or safety of an organization's information systems. When systems administrators know who is accessing a system and have defined what is normal behavior for that system, they are better able to determine when something is not right, and better able to determine if an anomaly should be elevated to the status of a potential security incident and forwarded to the incident response team for investigation. A digital security program must have comprehensive access control procedures and utilities in place. However, it must go well beyond that basic level of protection to prevent unauthorized or malicious intrusions where possible, and reduce the impact of intrusions and viruses when they occur. Various intrusion and virus detection techniques, such as gateway and content scanning, centralized logging, and antivirus programs, can help the reduce the risk of successful intrusion at points of entry and mitigate the consequences of intrusion events when they occur.

Intrusion and Virus Detection Techniques

Gateway scanning is a technique deployed to prevent unapproved or noncompliant attachments from entering a network or e-mail system by scanning the attachments.

Centralized logging is a technique deployed to facilitate the management of computer event logs. This technique involves systematically forwarding computer event logs to a single server, database, or system for storage and management.

Antivirus programs are software applications deployed to detect and remove malicious or problematic programs or utilities (viruses) from a computer, network, or system.

Content scanning is a technique deployed to scan network traffic with the goal of detecting Internet content that is not compliant with organizational policy.

Unauthorized or malicious intrusions and the dissemination of viruses can cause downtime, waste valuable resources for systems, and therefore personnel, and may cause damage or losses to sensitive, critical, or confidential data, cash, or other critical assets. Recent virus attacks, such as Nimda and Code Red (I and II), have shown not only how sophisticated cyber-threats have become, they have shown in dramatic ways just how vulnerable large systems are to such insidious attacks. Attacks can come in many forms and via many routes, and they create very different kinds of havoc on a system. The nature and number of threats "in the wild" are only two variables that make detecting, containing, and controlling the damage they inflict so difficult. Although the Code Reds and Nimda attacks were costly for many companies, there were remedies available. The most dangerous threat that any company can face is the one that it cannot contain or control. The impact of every other threat will be a matter of degree, which correlates directly to the organization's ability to deflect, contain, or control it. Therefore, the speed at which intrusions are detected directly impacts the ability to contain and control them.

Recent survey data indicates that external threats are a large cause of concern to organizations; however, external threats are actually less likely than threats that originate within the organization. If the chance of sustaining an internal threat is greater than an external threat, traditional intrusion detection measures, such as firewalls, virtual private networks (VPNs), or enhanced physical security, may not be enough because the intruder isn't an intruder at all but an otherwise authorized user. Highly effective intrusion and virus detection solutions can serve as indicators of imminent attack, and can be used in conjunction with a solid security policy and incident response program to respond in near real time to attacks in progress.

As shown in Figure 5.1, intrusion and virus detection is a central component of an aligned, proactive, and enterprise-wide digital security program. A properly designed intrusion and virus detection system is not product-focused, but is program-focused and employs many tools and techniques. It provides intrusion detection for all digital assets that could be targeted, such as the firewall, the router, the Web server, and the applications, and therefore functions as an early-warning tool. Functioning as a program, a well-designed intrusion detection system utilizes appropriate people and process components within an organiza-

FIGURE 5.1 The Intrusion and Virus Detection Framework

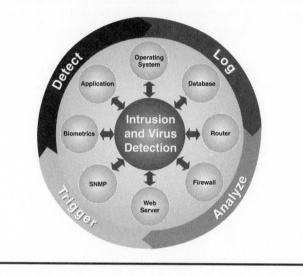

tion, not just the hardware, software, and other technological components. It provides guidance on the people component, such as policies, training, and certifications, and the process component, such as procedures, countermeasures, and standards, that will enable the organization's digital security team to detect, identify, and respond to intrusions, viruses, misuse, and policy violations in near real time. An intrusion and virus detection system that takes such an approach and is fully implemented will reduce downtime, mitigate real losses or damage, deflect damage done to intangible assets such as consumer confidence and corporate image, and maximize return on investment from security monitoring programs.

The planning team of a digital security program must possess capabilities that are key to initiating as well as maintaining the intrusion and virus detection system. Policies must be developed and maintained that establish management direction and objectives with regard to intrusion and virus detection. Business requirements must be determined and used to justify the deployment of intrusion and virus detection resources. Education requirements to design, operate, and monitor the system must be identified and provided to personnel responsible for initiating and maintaining intrusion and virus detection. Formal communications should be established that will reach the appropriate audiences and inform them about ongoing status and value provided by the system. Once established, policies, requirements, and education should be routinely assessed and appropriately updated according to

---

An Intrusion and Virus Detection Scenario

A global financial organization had deployed their intrusion and virus detection technology across several locations in the United States and Europe. Sensor systems were administered by regional personnel; however, there was no central point within the organization that collected and analyzed alerts. Late one evening, a computer worm began to infect several locations. The worm stole password files from infected machines and sent them to sites around the world. It also installed a distributed denial-of-service tool so that the infected machines could be used in denial-of-service attacks against other organizations. Since each site managed their own intrusion detection sensors, information was slow to reach the CIO and Director of IT Security. Before a decision could be made to block all outbound network activity to contain the worm, infected machines began to attack outside organizations. The event was reported by the news media, and the financial organization lost a significant amount of revenue and market share based on the event.

Summary: The distributed nature of digital environments demands polling and collection of network activity in a centralized, enterprise-wide fashion to facilitate control and containment of malicious network events that could significantly damage the organization. Although in this scenario each intrusion detection sensor effectively performed its core function, the lack of aligned business and security objectives caused the digital security program to fail. The lack of aggregation and centralized notification allowed the worm's malicious activity to compound its effect on the organization.

changing environmental conditions. Finally, project management for the deployment is provided to the organization.

The intrusion and virus detection system architecture team develops standards and guidelines for tools and processes. Technical requirements are mapped to business requirements, and technical designs of automated remedies are developed. Should the technical remedies require third-party software or services, RFPs are developed and published. The operations team implements the remedies. This implementation takes the form of deploying the countermeasures, maintaining awareness of the health of the altered component or system, taking input from vulnerability management to guide overall response, and continuously updating the intrusion and virus detection system to increase capacity for detection. Monitoring personnel track user movements and audit systems usage by manual and automated means, passing information about unauthorized activities to the incident response team for review, preventing potential incidents from occurring or initiated events from escalating.

Incident Response

Defining a security incident should be an easy thing to do. These days, everyone is familiar with the concept, if not the actions, of a hacker or a virus, and policy violations and denial-of-service attacks are fairly self-explanatory.[1] Then there are lesser known but widely occurring incidents such as unauthorized use of networks or systems for processing or storing information, attempts to gain unauthorized access to data or systems, and unauthorized attempts to change or delete information within a system. Accidents and oversights can't be ruled out either. New passwords get written down for the sake of convenience and are copied or stolen, an ex-employee retains access to systems after separating from the company, or sensitive or confidential data is erroneously posted to a web site and causes a financial or image crisis. All of these scenarios, and many more, can be classified as security incidents and the response in each situation must be fast and effective to contain the incident, prevent escalation, mitigate the damage already caused, and lessen the costs of repair and recovery.

As mentioned in Chapter 1, the most dangerous issues within the realm of digital security are threats and vulnerabilities. Threats to information systems may come in the form of an attack. An attack is *the exploitation of one or more vulnerabilities to cause the target system harm.* Information attacks most often serve as a means to an end and can be *active*, such as the introduction of a virus or worm, or *passive*, such as the interception of transmissions. The degree to which an attack succeeds is frequently in proportion to the opportunities afforded to adversaries by the targeted organization. Organizations that fail to protect their resources present adversaries with unlimited opportunities for attacks; those that exercise security due diligence can diminish that window of opportunity.

A **threat** to an information system is any act upon or against the system that is performed with the intention to cause harm.

A **vulnerability** is an inherent weakness within an information system.

Active Attacks

Perhaps the most recognized active attack is the *denial-of-service* attack, which is an orchestrated effort to deny service to an authorized user by overtaxing the resources of the system, thereby rendering it unable to respond to requests for service. Engagement in a denial-of-service attack on a high-profile web site is more often the means to an end rather than an end in itself. The desired outcome of such an attack may be decreased consumer confidence, public embarrassment, or diminished shareholder value. Potential adversaries who possess the requisite time, technology, and knowledge to orchestrate a denial-of-service attack need only to be willing to accept the subsequent risk of prosecution to successfully attack an organization with malicious intent.

Existing protection mechanisms put in place by a targeted organization may fail to prevent or compensate due to the distributed nature of such an attack. "Distributed" in this instance refers to source of the attack, which can and frequently does originate from multiple users with or without the knowledge of the user, as described in the scenario presented in the section on intrusion and virus detection. Software code containing instructions to commence a synchronized attack can be disseminated in much the same way a virus is disseminated, using automated propagation via e-mailed files, for instance, and the code can reside benignly and illicitly in a computer or a system unbeknownst to the user or owner.

Denial-of-service attacks gained popularity in the late 1990s with high-profile successes against recognized e-commerce leaders, such as Yahoo and eBay. According to the 2002 CSI/FBI survey, 40 percent of respondents had detected denial-of-service attacks in the previous 12 months,[2] with an average loss of just under $300,000.[3] In addition to denial-of-service attacks, adversaries may engage in theft of service, software modification, or other types of active systems attack. These may include viruses (replicating malicious instructions designed to be executed when triggered and which seek to infect information systems on a large scale), worms (malicious code that self-propagates through networks, causing damage along its path), or Trojan horses (programs, scripts, or files that contain malicious code and are triggered after they have penetrated perimeter defenses).

Passive Attacks

Passive attacks probably occur more frequently than active attacks, and the information gathered during a passive attack may fuel subsequent active attacks. However, passive attacks have an added element that makes them potentially more damaging than active attacks: An organization may be under passive attack for extended periods of time without realizing it because such activity produces little discernable data for systems administrators or security practitioners. (See the Low and Slow scenario in Chapter 7.) It is difficult to clearly estimate the percentage of passive attacks because the sheer volume of traffic on most networks precludes security, network, and systems administrators from collecting and analyzing the data necessary to indicate passive attack activities on a network.

In many cases, passive attacks are used to capture information that may embarrass an organization when made public. Passive attacks may take the form of *data interception*, or *sniffing*. This is accomplished through the use of a sniffer, a device that is used to assess network traffic. This is a widely accepted tool used by network and systems administrators for troubleshooting and for determining traffic flow, etc. Its use becomes less benign when applied to nonoperational or unauthorized uses, such as to copy data as it passes a node on a network so that the data can be collected in order to monitor organizational communications, or to identify potentially exploitable, high-value targets. Another utility widely used for routine and diagnostic purposes is *pinging*. This is a tool that sends a small message to a system to determine if the system is running. *Serial pinging*, which sends messages to many or all computers in a system within a highly compressed time frame, can effectively cause a network to lock up.

A highly effective digital security program will have in place continuous monitoring routines so that threats, vulnerabilities, and intrusions will be detected, which is a critical step that precedes and triggers an incident response. Without monitoring routines and policies that define a threat and provide instruction on how to proceed when encountering one, the entire organization may be at risk or even under attack for extended periods of time. This can entail vast real damages in terms of diminished productivity, lost or compromised data, and damaged or infected systems, and incalculable damage in terms of image, and consumer and shareholder confidence. In a worst-case scenario, the digital effectiveness of entire organization could be brought to a halt.

An effective Digital Security program must have in place incident response countermeasures that are understood by the entire enterprise and that have been practiced by the digital security team and allied personnel, such as systems and network administrators. A well-planned incident response program should ensure quick response, containment, and recovery times, and should include a multidisciplinary incident response team operating within a phased incident-handling approach. When a digital security program is aligned with business objectives, and has made enterprise-wide awareness of incident response counter-measures a priority it will have guidelines that enable incident response teams to be formed quickly according to the parameters of the incident. For example, an e-mail-borne virus attack that remains internal would require the expertise of security personnel as well as systems and net-work administrators. However, an attack or intrusion originating from a web site may require a team composed of systems, network, and secu-rity experts as well as web server personnel, perhaps public or media relations personnel if the attack is made public, and legal personnel if crimes were committed. Incident response teams should also be aware of assistance that can be obtained from external sources.

The purpose of an incident response program is to help protect and secure an organization's critical assets when they are compromised while maintaining close alignment with one of the organization's key business objectives: system availability. As shown in Figure 5.2, an effective inci-dent response program helps the organization contain and recover from computer security breaches and threats by leveraging continuous event detection and analysis countermeasures; it also provides input to those who administer and define the tools and processes that enable protec-tion, and does so in both reactive and proactive ways. Functions that may be considered part of the incident response program include secu-rity awareness training, intrusion detection, documentation, penetration testing, or even program development. These proactive capabilities can help an organization prevent computer security incidents, and decrease the response time involved when an incident occurs.

There are two major aspects of the incident response program: the event life cycle and the program life cycle. The methodology of the program life cycle is that program objectives are defined, possible solu-tions are analyzed, capabilities are identified, and the incident response agenda item is designed and implemented. Administration of the agenda

FIGURE 5.2　　The Incident Response Framework

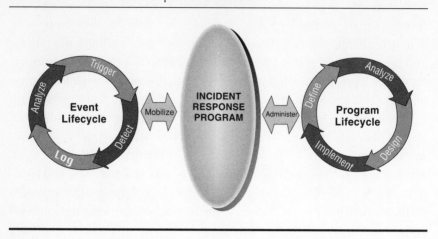

item will indicate new objectives, which in turn will drive the cycle to begin again.

The event life cycle is also continuous and plays out for every incident or event incurred. An event triggers the mobilization process, which begins with detecting and logging the event. Analysis leads to decisions that enable control and containment. The analysis may also lead to the definition of new objectives, which in turn lead to alterations to the deployment strategy of the incident response agenda item.

Assessing and absorbing the costs of damage inflicted during an attack is a painful process; bearing exorbitant response and recovery costs due to inadequate preparation is adding insult to injury. A well-planned, proactive, and formal incident response program can reduce the clean-up costs of a security incident. An organization with such a program in place will initiate preplanned routines when the incident is detected. Countermeasures to control damage and contain escalation will commence, and recovery processes will be set in motion according to preexisting policies that allow non-security personnel to return their focus to core competencies, and do so quickly.

The right program will reduce time and costs associated with incident response and recovery by analyzing, upgrading, formalizing, and validating response capabilities; providing consistent, repeatable methods and processes; and employing the leading technologies. It will define and implement tools and technologies that can reduce the time required to analyze and respond to incidents. It will also validate the organization's current incident response capabilities and formalize the appropriate incident response processes and procedures necessary to align the program with strategic business objectives.

Planning capabilities for incident response are key to initiating as well as maintaining a program. Policies must be established that develop and maintain management direction and objectives. Policies that govern roles and responsibilities for incident response must also be developed. For example, it is through these executive-sponsored policies that production systems can be taken offline if such an action is deemed necessary to contain an incident. Business requirements for incident response are determined and used to justify the deployment of resources. Education requirements to execute the program must be identified and provided to appropriate personnel. Documentation procedures, which detail ongoing status and the value provided by incident response, must be established and distributed to appropriate personnel for initiation and maintenance. All of these efforts are continuously reviewed and updated as conditions warrant.

The architecture team must have the capability to develop standards and guidelines for incident response tools and processes. Any technical requirements are mapped to the business requirements and technical designs, and process flows of automated fixes are developed. RFPs are developed and published if technical remedies require third-party software or services.

The operations team identifies and deploys the appropriate resources to contain the incident and mitigate any impacts. Then the team implements the systemic or incident-specific repairs and accompanying processes, assesses the health of the revised component or system, provides training and awareness, and conducts forensic investigations as appropriate.

An Incident Response Scenario

A global manufacturing organization had never fully developed a formal incident response process and team. The organization's IT division did not feel the need to expend time and resources in developing this kind of capability; they had never been "hacked" during their 27 years of existence. Then, on a weekend afternoon in June, a hacker penetrated the organization's network, stole password files, installed back doors, and downloaded confidential information about the company. Once the hacker obtained access to the internal network, his activities traversed the entire corporation across all geographical locations. As administrators were alerted around the United States and the Far East, the hacker began to divert his activities to other targets using the company's compromised systems as launching points. He left the organization's network when he became aware that administrators were trying to track his activity.

Chaos and confusion marked the first 48 hours of the attack. Some administrators were unequipped to respond to the attack. Others, who were equipped to respond to compromised systems, did so in a variety of ways. The review and triage of log information was performed by several administrators independently, which meant senior management was unable to get an overall view of the state of security of the network, and the systems review procedures applied were inconsistent with established computer forensics procedures. Therefore, any potential evidence discovered would have been considered questionable in a court proceeding. The net result of the incident was that the incident cost the organization several hundred thousand dollars in remediation, and the hacker was never identified despite leaving numerous footprints of his activities on the network.

Summary: This incident is a classic study in how to do everything wrong. By relying on history and statistical probability, the organization chose to follow an ad hoc, reactive approach rather than a formal, proactive approach by not installing preventive systems across the enterprise. Because no formal communications structure or hierarchy existed and there was no validated reporting system in place, redundant and incomplete information was disseminated, which further hindered the recovery effort.

Malicious network activity often happens quickly, without warning, and puts company assets and brand at risk. It can also create the perception of lack of due diligence if the compromised network is used as a launching point to attack other organizations. Effective control and containment requires a formal, trained incident response team that operates within distinct guidelines, follows accepted procedures, continually exercises its methodologies and updates them as necessary, and has the ability and authority to make time-sensitive decisions on behalf of the organization. The alternative, a team formed on an ad hoc or as needed basis, leads to an incomplete and poor response effort.

Privacy

Conducting business in today's connected economy means facing complex privacy issues that affect operations at all levels, including information systems. How an organization chooses to address privacy will determine whether its privacy policies are a competitive advantage or a potential risk. Business, technical, reputation, and regulatory risks associated with privacy must be determined, and organizations must balance these risks with the need to maximize the utility of the information they possess while building trust and confidence among stakeholders.

Because organizations now have the ability to collect vast amounts of data regarding individuals and limitless capacity to store it, developing, implementing, and maintaining privacy programs have become highly debated issues in legislative halls and subsequently in boardrooms worldwide. The convenience of global interconnectivity has its risks, because dependence on digital systems increases the potential for successful penetrations of vulnerable or unsecured systems. Privacy concerns related to the gathering, storage, and use of information can affect custodial organizations on many levels, and breaches of privacy—whether due to policies not being followed, intrusion incidents, or simply errors—can cause significant damage to image, brand, market share, and shareholder and consumer confidence. Similarly, noncompliance with laws and regulations can initiate fines and, in some instances, failure to protect privacy can be legally actionable. It is critical, therefore, that executive management understands the risks of increased connectivity with regard to privacy issues.

This is a key reason why organizations with digital security programs in place self-regulate their privacy initiatives, embrace third-party verification of their processes and technology, and have a formal privacy risk management program sponsored at the executive level. Such programs identify risks associated with privacy and help to ensure that the organization's privacy countermeasures are conducted in accordance with fair information practices as well as within regulatory and legal guidelines. An organization's privacy policies must address the entire enterprise, which, as defined in Chapter 2, includes business partners both upstream and downstream and the entities those partners entrust with critical information and organizational security.

A digital security program must include an understanding of and commitment to privacy. It should include personnel responsible for identifying, interpreting, and applying new and existing laws and regulations that affect the organization. It should have in place policies and procedures that drive compliance with those mandates, as well as technical solutions that enable compliance. The policies must be documented and communicated to all departments and groups that work with covered information; policies must also be mapped to appropriate systems. If these basic safeguards are implemented, simply executing the digital security program will keep privacy concerns in check.

Policies that address issues across the enterprise and at all levels must be developed, and management must take them into account when issuing decisions and directives regarding business objectives. For example, establishing World Wide Web-based database applications or interactive web sites may require additional security precautions and countermeasures to ensure a higher level of user authentication. Roles and responsibilities ranging from the individual to the organizational level must be established and codified in policies as well. Business requirements must drive the deployment of resources with regard to compliance with privacy requirements, for instance, the creation of an executive-level privacy officer. Risk assessments must be conducted to determine which digital assets may be in need of privacy controls. Once established, compliance should be routinely reviewed and appropriately updated, with incidents of noncompliance documented via a waiver framework.

The architecture team develops standards and guidelines for privacy-related tools and processes. Often, technical solutions are needed to provide the level controls needed to ensure privacy compliance, for instance on systems that are physically and logically disconnected from others. Business and technical requirements must be aligned and mapped, and technical designs of automated solutions developed. Any waivers should be analyzed to determine whether solutions exist or extensions to the technical security architecture need to be developed. Ultimately, security architects are tasked to incorporate and apply technological solutions that will appropriately lessen the chance that unauthorized persons will gain access to private information.

The operations team ensures that standards are deployed in accordance with the policies for keeping private information private, and for maintaining access privileges to restricted systems or areas. The operations team is also responsible for ensuring that such standards and policies are understood, implemented, and followed. This capability also entails continuous review of systems' status with respect to policies to ensure continued compliance as changes are made to federal, state, and local laws, as well as internal or industry requirements. Privacy training and awareness programs are presented to ensure that employees understand the importance of privacy and know what tools are at their disposal for maintaining appropriate levels of privacy. Any technical solutions that enable privacy protection must be in accordance with policy.

The monitoring team supports the operations team by ensuring that procedures for access to private information are followed, and that systems remain secure and are monitored for unauthorized use or transactions. These tasks include the following activities: conducting system audits, gathering information for compliance reporting, reviewing pertinent investigation outcomes, and if needed, assisting with any response to incidents concerning privacy.

Privacy Scenario

A leading cable company with millions of subscribers started collecting detailed information about its subscribers' Web surfing habits. When this became known, consumers, civil liberty groups, and privacy advocates became outraged and filed a class-action lawsuit demanding monetary compensation for violations of privacy rights. Although only a subset of subscribers was being monitored, the cable company may face damages in the millions of dollars.

Summary: If the company had proactively created a privacy policy that clearly defined parameters for collecting and using subscriber information and formally communicated that policy throughout the enterprise, the business unit executive who made the decision to collect subscriber information would have been aware of the possible consequences and impact of that decision on the business objectives of the organization. Had the same decision been made despite the policy directive, a validated and continuously monitored privacy program would have alerted personnel that information was being collected in violation of the privacy policy.

Organizations are at risk on both sides of this issue. Litigation related to privacy issues is increasing at an alarming rate worldwide, and the monetary damages are substantial, resulting in higher insurance costs. On the other side of the issue, privacy-related regulations are constantly being modified and enhanced, making it imperative that an organization's privacy program is continuously monitored and upgraded to reflect those changes. It is the responsibility of executive management to ensure that those privacy policies are clearly defined, communicated, followed, and monitored.

Policies, Standards, and Guidelines

There are no rules that hackers follow. Their motivations vary but their basic methodology does not: They find a vulnerability, and they exploit it. An organization may not know it is a target until it has become a victim, and this, in part, is why defending against an attack is so difficult. It is why the organization must develop its own rules of engagement if none exist. No one in an organization can know where or how or when the next attack will occur, but an executive-sponsored, appropriately funded digital security team can and will determine what needs to be defended and how best to institute an effective defense. The first step that team must take is to put in place the policies, standards, and guidelines agenda item, which enables an organization to proactively plan, manage, and respond to information security risks, threats, and vulnerabilities.

The executive managers of organizations with digital security programs in place understand that policy is the communication link between business operations and IT support. They also understand that formal rules of engagement that are documented, distributed, and implemented are essential to ensure compliance by all of the organization's personnel. The rules of engagement must include policies that are measurable and attainable, and supported by both configuration standards and behavioral guidelines. They define issues, roles, and responsibilities, effectively setting the bar for the digital security program as a whole, and this clarity enables personnel to weigh risks as acceptable or unacceptable. Without formal, proactive, comprehensive security documentation that instructs and guides behavior and decisions, it is virtually impossible for an organization to effectively manage and protect its digital resources. The three parts of this agenda item are further defined as follows:

- *Policies* define roles and responsibilities, state management direction, and provide for waiver documentation. How organizations determine domains of coverage for security policies is often as unique as their business model. Some choose to identify and conform to a recognized standard. Adherence to a recognized information security standard, such as International Standards Organization (ISO) 17799, provides additional credibility for a security program, and may continually serve as a compliance goal for security practitioners.
- *Standards* identify minimum security configurations for digital assets, are detailed and typically focus on specific technologies and/or explicitly clarify vague policies.
- *Guidelines* provide direction to the organization with respect to approaching digital security in specific situations or scenarios. Guidelines

may be appropriate when there are more than one or two acceptable solutions for a particular digital security challenge, or they may evolve into specific policies, procedures, or standards as needed.

As presented in Figure 5.3, ensuring that an organization's documentation suite is comprehensive and effective requires periodic reassessment and review, as does every functioning segment of a digital security system. Regulations and industry standards change, business practices and objectives are modified, the economy strengthens and weakens cyclically, new malware (malicious code) and methods of digital attack are developed, and all of these, as well as other events, can affect the utility and applicability of an organization's policies, standards, and guidelines program. An organization with a fully deployed policies, standards, and guidelines program in place will absorb and address such changes. The personnel required to carry out the update process are sponsored at the executive level. They understand both the organization's business objectives and its risk with regard to digital security, as

---

FIGURE 5.3   The Policies, Standards, and Guidelines Framework[4]

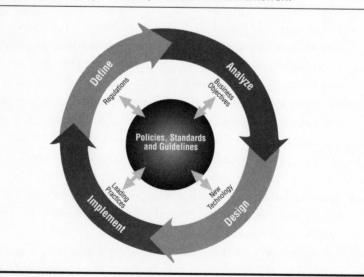

well as how policy modifications may affect those objectives. When the review and validation process is complete, the updated policies are communicated throughout the organization in a timely and efficient manner.

Executive management must support the development and implementation of digital security policies, thereby establishing the charter for the digital security program and lending it authority. Only with the unambiguous support of senior management can such a program become effective, useful, and functional. Once it becomes functional, its value can be established and understood. It is through execution of the four core capabilities of planning, architecture, operations, and monitoring that a digital security program applies the policies, standards, and guidelines it has adopted.

Personnel responsible for planning digital security draft policies based on need and/or direction from management. Management sets this direction in accordance with governance responsibilities. Policies are formally communicated to the organization and affect how digital security functional groups, such as incident response teams and network personnel, deliver their services. Deviations from policies are documented via a waiver process, and accountability is established for risk acceptance and mitigation.

One of the core responsibilities of the digital security architecture team is mapping policies to standards and guidelines. Standards and guidelines affect how the architects choose to design and implement digital security solutions for the organization. Any policy waivers are analyzed to determine the feasibility of mitigating deviations through technical solutions.

The operations team relies upon formal policies, standards, and guidelines for direction and support in conducting digital security operations on a day-to-day basis. Operations personnel apply security configurations based on standards and guidelines; perform account, vulnerability, and entitlement management routines; and communicate status according to established policies. Status of operations is reported to the planning personnel to be communicated formally to the appropriate management audiences. Training and awareness activities equip the general population of employees with the ability to make good decisions regarding digital security while performing their everyday duties. For example, deploying operating system patches to contain any prevalent worm viruses is a common practice. The ability of the operations team to efficiently deploy these patches is critical to containing the spread and continuation of virus infections, and having the current standards—in this case, the patches—deployed on systems improves the ability of an organization's systems to prevent intrusion and virus incidents proactively. Other operations activities include system repair, reassessment of the security measures for that system or component, and follow-through.

The monitoring team relies on policies, standards, and guidelines to direct the methodology, frequency, and level of detail in its reporting on the state of digital security on a day-to-day basis. Monitoring personnel observe systems to determine trends and anomalies, conduct security audits, gauge system compliance, and, if needed, assist with response to incidents related to policies, standards, and guidelines.

A Policy, Standards, and Guidelines Scenario

Recently, an organization discovered that an employee was using a company server in a test lab to download music files for personal use after hours. Although the employee had no malicious intent, he was unaware that his downloads were taking up network bandwidth and causing significant delays in testing a critical software package. The employee was reprimanded but not disciplined because the company had no formal policy that addressed the use of company equipment by employees for personal business. There were no guidelines that made employees aware of the implications of using company equipment for personal use or policies that identified punitive actions for employees who abused company equipment or privileges.

Summary: The process of creating and formalizing organizational policies, standards, and guidelines requires that organizations define their digital security posture and define how the digital security program will be implemented across the organization. Organizations without formal digital security policies in place will lack direction regarding their digital security posture and, in some cases, will lack the ability to hold employees accountable for their actions.

Physical Security

Locks, bars, alarms, and uniformed guards are what many people associate with the concept of security. Such measures are fundamental to an organization's total security effort because if the physical security of a facility or organization is in doubt or in jeopardy, all other efforts become significantly more difficult to initiate and deploy. When considering the framework of a digital security program, physical security is often overlooked. However, it is a key component of controlling access to digital assets. Physical security efforts are often managed and directed parallel to but not in conjunction with the management and direction of digital security operations. This lack of proactive, enterprise-wide cohesion can lead to a situation in which the physical security measures that are intended to support the digital security program are out of alignment with actual needs and requirements.

Protecting employees and company assets from unforeseen dangers and unpredictable occurrences is of increasing importance for senior management, and physical security has become a fundamental component of overall corporate security. Appropriate building construction, adequate and consistent power supplies, reliable climate control, and effective protection from intruders are some of the issues that must be addressed when considering the security of buildings, infrastructure, and equipment, as well as of the information and systems contained therein. As organizations continue to seek digital solutions to increase productivity, one side effect has been the introduction of additional challenges to managing physical security. For example, as the use of VPNs and wireless LANs has become more common in the workplace and larger numbers of employees are working from remote offices, physical security plans must be adapted to account for more and more digital assets being operated outside the traditional, controlled, hard-wired environment of the corporate office. It is only when physical and digital security programs are aligned that organizations can effectively manage risks to digital assets.

As shown in Figure 5.4, an aligned physical and digital security effort will be coordinated at all levels and will ensure there are regularly

FIGURE 5.4 The Physical Security Framework

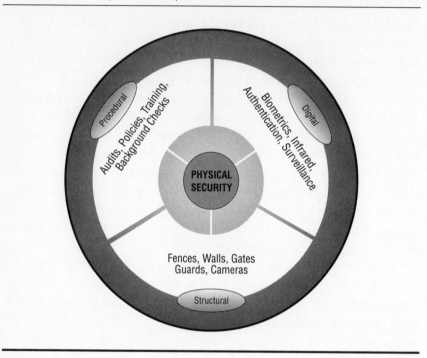

scheduled communications between the digital security team and the physical security team. The physical security team must have an understanding of digital security issues and adjust accordingly. For example, the use of automated systems for performing background checks or the introduction of digital surveillance or access control applications may require cooperative training between the teams. The physical security team will play a critical role in the execution of any disaster recovery and business continuity plans, and therefore it must be involved in their development and a participant in corresponding exercises. Finally, regular testing of physical security controls that are in place can provide a benchmark and subsequently indicate how successfully the physical security program is executing.

Careful planning will streamline and enhance the integration of physical and digital security measures. Corporate security is most effective when the physical and logical flow of people, information, and materials through corporate facilities is understood holistically rather than as separate concerns and separate systems. Business goals and objectives and management concerns play a large role in developing policies that address physical security issues. Everything from the geographical location of offices to data center security and hardware protection to offsite data storage facilities, as well as the responsibilities and obligations of individuals, must be taken into account when crafting such policies. For example, organizations may need to educate employees across the enterprise as to the importance of clear-desk policies and screensaver password policies. It may need to install locks for laptops or institute the use of removable, classified hard drives. Deployment of physical security resources must be in alignment with business requirements as well as actual needs. Such needs can only be determined by conducting risk assessments to determine which digital assets may be in need of physical security controls.

The architecture team can bridge the gap between the digital and the physical aspects of security. Standards and guidelines for implementing physical security policies must be developed. Technical solutions may be required to automate the implementation of some of the policies. For instance, if an organization has determined that biometric countermeasures are needed to achieve the desired level of security, the architecture team is tasked with carrying out deployment. This includes determining which method will best meet the organizational requirements, for instance, voice, retinal, or fingerprint recognition. It also includes determining the parameters of the system, purchasing and deploying the software and hardware, and configuring and validating the system.

The operations team must be closely aligned with physical security efforts to enforce the countermeasures that have been instituted to provide a secure environment for digital assets, such as handling situations when computers have been left accessible and unattended or media, such as floppy disks or CDs, have been left unsecured. The operations team also supports and carries out security awareness programs and provides training for new systems and countermeasures.

The monitoring team also supports an aligned physical security effort, particularly with regard to auditing aspects. Policies, standards, and guidelines include physical protection of digital assets, and the monitoring team is responsible for conducting audits to ensure compliance. Audits conducted to ensure that physical security policies are followed can identify gaps that may lead to strengthening policies, standards, and guidelines.

A Physical Security Scenario

Several years ago, a large university in the Midwest was the target of an attack by a disgruntled computer science student. The student manifested his anger with the school by entering the computer facility with a handful of magnet filings, and proceeded to disable a mainframe that contained all student records. Although the act was simple, it was extremely effective. Rather than risk exposing the backup tapes to the filings and suffering a total loss of the data, the decision was made to keep the systems down until replacement hardware could be found. Recovering this security breach took weeks of waiting for the equipment as well hundreds of man-hours to repair and restore critical systems.

Summary: Even though access to the university's buildings and facilities was limited to students and staff, proper physical security countermeasures were not in place to prevent access to critical information systems. This "hard crunchy outside and soft chewy center" is not uncommon among organizations, that have yet to accept that threats exist internally as well as externally. This example underscores the importance of applying measures throughout the enterprise and not just at the perimeter to create a secure environment.

RUN

As described above, when an organization has set the parameters of its digital security initiatives by crafting and implementing policies, standards, and guidelines, it has begun a process that will enable it to achieve proactive stability in the face of threats and vulnerabilities. An organization that has reinforced those parameters by instituting counter-measures such as intrusion and virus detection mechanisms and privacy programs, and has achieved a level of security by having enterprise-wide physical security and incident response systems in place, has built a strong foundation for a world-class digital security program. Such a program can move to the next level of achieving digital security, which entails managing the interior components of the organization: its assets, its vulnerabilities, and its system privileges.

The foundation of implementing a world-class digital security program is securing the organization's digital assets by restricting their availability to persons who have an established need for having access to them and prohibiting access by all others. Enabling an organization to identify and maintain a balance in restricting access to digital assets requires having mechanisms in place that allow the organization to function fluidly within a secure environment by ensuring protections at a higher level. These protections must also serve to reinforce the alignment between the organization's business and security objectives.

The next sections introduce items within the Run agenda. These agenda items are methodologies that address securing and managing organizational assets, assessing and managing vulnerabilities; and granting and revoking privileges. Maintaining appropriate access privileges is a balancing act. If access is limited too severely, functionality is compromised; if access is not controlled tightly enough, security is compromised. The degree to which an organization's private information must be protected can change over time or upon reaching financial or other milestones. The need for access also changes frequently within organizations as projects begin and end and employees are hired, change positions within the firm, and separate from the firm. Therefore, determining who is given authorized access, when, and why can be a decision fraught with fine lines and minute distinctions, and it is frequently addressed in terms of the principle of least privilege. This principle states that users of digital information should be granted only the level of access to information required to perform their jobs and no more.

Asset and Service Management

Productivity is and always has been the goal of any business organization. Any mechanism, procedure, or technology that may improve productivity is assessed in terms of its potential utility and return on investment. The increasing costs and complexities of maintaining employee workspace have elevated the importance of implementing new methods of managing assets effectively and securely while improving productivity and accountability. These aligned objectives can be achieved by executing an integrated and comprehensive asset and service management program, which may include help-desk functions, detailed asset repositories, change management processes, and self-service functions.

Asset management involves more than maintaining equipment inventories and software licensing documentation. It is a comprehensive approach to managing all of an organization's assets: infrastructure, physical components, digital data, and intangibles. Assets that are overlooked or not accounted for can be problematic to the balance sheet in many ways. A laptop that is not accounted for and not being maintained and upgraded with security patches can become a breeding ground for vulnerabilities. For example, if the laptop has a connection to a rogue modem, it can be an entry point for an outside intruder, or it may have been compromised by a sleeper program, which can be used to launch a future attack. The financial and reputational aftermath of such a situation can be significant.

Effective asset management at an enterprise level must be sponsored at the executive level. It involves input from financial, information technology, procurement, human resources, and other areas in the organization, and takes into account such things as lease management, order management, and asset tracking at the user level. It better enables organizations to understand their assets and their total cost of ownership. When designed and implemented appropriately, an asset management program incorporates the people, process, and technology drivers with a management process to provide clear information that enables an organization to properly manage and track its assets, and the cost of those assets. The result is a reinforced, enterprise-wide digital security program.

A well-designed and fully implemented asset and service management program will show real benefits that can be measured in real terms. Efficiencies achieved across the enterprise include increased productivity for IT personnel and those relying on them, as well as reduced downtime of assets and improved customer service. Knowing what assets the organization possesses, where they are, and who is accountable for them is essential for those tasked with effectively managing digital security. Also, this information contributes toward cost reductions and return on investment because tracked assets can be redeployed more quickly, resulting in less redundancy and enabling consolidation of maintenance contracts.

The Planning team for an asset and service management program requires a detailed understanding of the existing work flows, authorizations, and integration as a precursor to crafting policies that will support executive management-sponsored business objectives. Defining requirements for the future asset management process from procurement to retirement and understanding the digital assets that organizations deploy are prerequisites to conducting risk assessments and establishing critical pieces of policy related to where those assets physically and logically reside and operate. Education programs for individuals and groups responsible for assets, including those used offsite, must be developed.

The architecture team works to create and maintain security standards and guidelines after determining what physical and technological assets must be protected. The architecture team must be aware of what technology is available, must understand how it will be deployed, and must understand what it looks like from an enterprise perspective to ensure that the technical designs and systems architecture planned can scale to adequate levels. After completing this technology survey, the architecture team designs the asset management system structure, building in the appropriate depth, breadth, and flexibility required by the organization. This can include defining user and privilege profiles, constructing databases using appropriate and integrated software tools, determining naming conventions and data classifications, and constructing procedures for data migration. The architecture must provide security for assets at all levels and functions and enable enhanced business performance.

The operations team must have the capability to deploy and implement the formalized, established standards and guidelines developed for digital assets, and to continuously monitor those assets to maintain efficiency and consistency across the enterprise. This can include both manual and automated tasks such as setting up and maintaining user accounts, identifying assets as enduring or consumable, and ensuring that inventory control stickers are placed on appropriate assets. From a service management perspective, the operations team can leverage the capabilities of the organization to coordinate communications and facilitate some aspects of digital security reporting. This facilitation could be in the way of leased service management staff or even assignment of specific security operations staff to perform some duties alongside the traditional service management team. Training and security awareness programs are implemented enterprise-wide.

The actions taken by the monitoring team are the final stage in enabling the success of an asset and service management program. Monitoring personnel must know the specific types of assets that are being monitored to understand where the sensitive or critical information resides and to better understand what activities are authorized or not authorized while conducting their monitoring. This capability supports the secure operations of an organization by permitting hard assets to be tracked for inventory control and financial reasons. It also allows access to easily compromised assets, such as digital information, to be audited for user compliance. From a service management perspective, the monitoring team can leverage the capabilities of the organization to coordinate communications and facilitate some aspects of digital security intrusion and virus detection.

> ### An Asset and Service Management Scenario
>
> During regularly scheduled maintenance of its digital assets, a major retailer discovered a potent virus resident in its systems. The virus was intended to deploy across the organization's systems on the day before Thanksgiving, and its payload would effectively destroy the functionality of every cash register. The virus was neutralized and a catastrophic event averted because of the integrated actions of the organization's asset management and incident response teams. The subsequent forensic investigation revealed that a disgruntled employee had deployed the virus.
>
> **Summary:** Although the outcome of this incident was positive, the reality is that this situation could have been avoided entirely had there been a proactive, enterprise-wide digital security program in place. Such a program would have prevented unauthorized access by the employee into such a critical system. If the employee was authorized for that system, change control and monitoring applications would have issued alerts regarding system changes, and the insertion of the malware into the system would have triggered the intrusion and virus detection system.

Vulnerability Management

Thousands of vulnerabilities and associated exploitations are introduced into information systems each year. Disparate systems, platforms, and applications contribute to the difficulty of tracking new vulnerabilities and ensuring system integrity. Therefore, appropriate safeguards and potential points of failure must be addressed on an enterprise-wide level. A formal vulnerability management program offers organizations an integrated solution that provides for centralized monitoring and automated methods of ensuring that compliance and secure configurations are maintained throughout the organization. Taking this type of proactive approach can result in significant incident response cost savings and an improved security posture.

An effective defense against unknown vulnerabilities can only be established when digital security decision makers have a detailed understanding of the organization's system and significant environmental vulnerabilities. This knowledge must be expanded as threats change, which is to say constantly, and the new knowledge must be acted upon. Information about vulnerabilities and threats must be disseminated to the appropriate people, decisions must be made, precautions must be taken, and the results must be validated. Building accountability into the vulnerability management program is key to its effectiveness.

Vulnerabilities Within Information Systems

System vulnerabilities can include software bugs, which are inherent flaws in the code that cause systems to perform in unintended ways; unsecured ports of entry, such as Web servers; and back doors into systems, which allow or enable unauthorized activity. Physical vulnerabilities include unsecured printer locations or computer rooms; antiquated fire systems that will unnecessarily damage equipment while responding to an incident; inadequate or unreliable backup systems; inadequate infrastructure controls such as power backups and climate control; and inadequate offsite transport and storage practices.

The importance of having in place a vulnerability management program can be summed up in an easily understood figure: $17.11 billion.[5] This is the estimate of damage worldwide in 2000 from viruses and other malicious code attacks; in 1995, the figure was $0.5 billion.[6] The Love Bug virus that attacked organizations worldwide in 2000 caused $8.75 billion in damage by itself, and the Code Red viruses that attacked companies around the world in 2001 caused $2.62 billion in damage.[7] These viruses exploited known system and code vulnerabilities, which means that much of the damage inflicted could have been prevented had the organizations known about the vulnerabilities and acted on that knowledge.

The vulnerability management agenda item is an enterprise-wide progression of protection that moves outward to expand the security of critical information and infrastructures. As progress is made and the program is strengthened, the vulnerability management program enables the organization to track the status of vulnerabilities in real time by deploying appropriate controls, and to mitigate other vulnerabilities to the level of compliance with standards and regulations. Having in place broad, proactive methodologies to determine, deflect, and defuse security vulnerabilities means fewer incidents will occur, and experiencing fewer incidents translates into less downtime, which means strong tangible and intangible returns on investment in a marketplace under near-continual digital threat.

The planning capabilities for a digital security program rely heavily on the information contained within a vulnerability management system. Understanding vulnerabilities present in digital assets that organizations deploy is a prerequisite to crafting policies and conducting risk assessments. These tasks are critical to establishing programs to educate the organizational population as to the importance of implementing and following behavioral and logical safeguards. Documentation procedures that detail ongoing status and waiver policies that detail the exceptions must be developed and distributed to appropriate personnel for initiation and maintenance. All of these efforts are continuously reviewed and updated as conditions warrant. Business requirements must reflect the need for and importance of appropriate resource deployment, and project management must be initiated at suitable levels.

The architecture team must know what vulnerabilities exist to ensure that the technical design solutions created are more than adequate to protect current technological assets and the information they contain. Using policies already in place, the architecture team creates security standards and guidelines tailored to the vulnerability management system as a prerequisite to determining how technology must be protected. Business and technical requirements must be aligned and mapped, and technical designs of automated solutions developed. Waivers should be analyzed to determine whether solutions exist or extensions to the technical security architecture need to be developed. After the information-gathering phase has been completed, the team works to identify, design, and deploy technical solutions that support business objectives.

The operations team implements the standards and guidelines developed for digital assets and continuously monitors those assets for configuration consistency. This is where the day-to-day vulnerability management takes place. Vulnerabilities identified for existing and new digital assets must be recognized, investigated, validated, and communicated across the program to ensure that policies, standards, and guidelines drive the mitigation of risk associated with those vulnerabilities. Education and awareness programs are implemented.

Monitoring personnel must know vulnerabilities that are both present (where risk has been accepted) as well as those that have been or

A Vulnerability Management Scenario

Vulnerabilities come from many different directions. Hardware and software manufacturers may issue patches to fix newly discovered vulnerabilities in their systems. Many private and public organizations issue alerts and notices about vulnerabilities every day. Organizations need to understand these vulnerabilities, identify those that apply to their organization, and develop a process to apply these vulnerabilities to their environment. Any missed vulnerability can potentially expose your organization for an attack. Overlooking one low-priority vulnerability may not harm your organization, but a combination of several such overlooked vulnerabilities could cripple an organization.

Viruses such as Code Red and Nimda exploited several known vulnerabilities that many organizations classified as low-priority and did not patch. Therefore, many organizations were unprepared for the viruses' ultimate impact. Organizations that had implemented a good vulnerability management program and had evaluated the potential impact of not addressing these vulnerabilities were able to analyze the potential impact, apply to their assets the proper fixes to these vulnerabilities, and eliminate many hours of unproductive time, resulting in potential savings of millions.

Summary: Without an effective digital security program built around vulnerability management, organizations are more exposed to persons seeking to exploit vulnerabilities. A proactive vulnerability management program can eliminate many hours of potential downtime, resulting in no interruption to the business.

should have been addressed. Information about the current state of vulnerabilities in the environment is crucial to everyday monitoring activities. For that reason, the organization's monitoring capabilities must include appropriate levels of systems auditing activities to determine and support compliance and to determine changes in the vulnerability of organizational systems.

Entitlement Management

Trust is a basic requirement in any digital transaction. The customer or client must trust that the organization will take appropriate measures to safeguard private information, and executive management must trust that the digital security personnel understand the importance of security measures from a business as well as technological perspective. The loss of consumer trust can have a tremendous impact on an organization's image and brand and, therefore, on its bottom line. Establishing trust in a digital environment requires the use of the authorization and authentication procedures introduced in Chapter 3. When such techniques are properly deployed, they provide a strong foundation for digital defense. However, when poorly deployed, these techniques impart significant vulnerabilities to an organization's IT systems, which can lead to exploitation, unauthorized access, lost data, unnecessary downtime, or other disruptions. Entitlement management is the security agenda item that addresses this critical element of digital security.

As presented in Figure 5.5, adequate access and permission controls affect many interrelated organizational systems. The need to effectively administer user access is critical to every level of a digital security program. As an organization's dependency on digital technology expands and the user base increases in many sectors, including employees, customers, suppliers, and business partners, the challenge of supporting cost-effective, secure user administration activities becomes greater as well. A standard framework for centrally directed entitlement management must be established and communicated to the organization. A properly designed and deployed entitlement management program

FIGURE 5.5

operates to control access to systems and to authenticate the identities of authorized users. These controls must be deployed enterprise-wide and must operate proactively and continuously to reduce threats. When fully deployed and supported by formal policies and guidelines, such a program will reduce operating costs, increase productivity, and improve business management. Leading software companies are beginning to take an enterprise view of agenda items like entitlement management; see, for example, Computer Associates' approach to the Identity Lifecycle, depicted in Figure 5.6.

The planning capabilities of a digital security program set the direction for entitlement management and are key to initiating as well as maintaining the program. Policies that address issues across the enterprise and at all levels must be developed, and executive management must take them into account when issuing decisions and directives regarding business objectives. For example, policies are crafted to ensure that user identities are authenticated accurately and user authorizations are applied and removed in accordance with other corporate policies. Roles and responsibilities ranging from the individual to the organizational level must be established and codified in formal policies as well. Business requirements must drive the deployment of resources, and risk assessments must be conducted to determine if certain digital

FIGURE 5.6 Computer Associates' Model of Enterprise Identity Framework

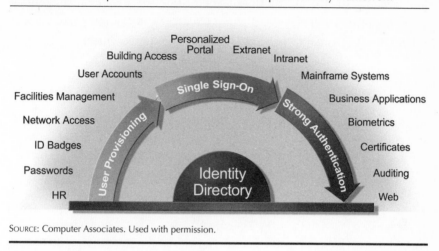

Source: Computer Associates. Used with permission.

assets may be in need of more stringent controls. Education programs must be established that will effectively communicate both the policies and need for them to the corporate populace. Compliance should be routinely reviewed and policies appropriately updated as business requirements change and technology advances.

As it works to identify, design, and deploy technical solutions, the architecture team must provide the leadership to ensure that the complexities of the technical architecture for entitlement management are integrated and scalable. Standards and guidelines must be developed that incorporate policy directives while supporting and enhancing business performance. Full functionality must be considered and tested prior to adoption.

The operations team directs the day-to-day entitlement management activities. Training and awareness programs are carried out, and the ultimate responsibility for entitlement management and account management resides with this group. Statistics regarding solution performance should be reported to management as a part of every-day digital security reporting.

Monitoring personnel are tasked with capturing user information and analyzing it for unusual behavior of the entitlement management item. Personnel will also conduct audits leveraging systems and tools to measure compliance to policies, standards, and guidelines.

An Entitlement Management Scenario

Authentication enables identity to be assigned to an individual within an organization. Through authentication, trust is established. With this trust, organizations can authorize individuals to access digital assets. If this trust is violated, a user could cause significant damage to an organization's digital assets.

The majority of organizations perform authentication based on an identification (called a user ID, sign-on ID, or logon ID) and a password. As business functions grow, the assignments of these IDs and passwords grow as well. When a user of the business is assigned multiple IDs and passwords (primarily because different technologies have different requirements for the way the IDs and passwords can be defined), they tend to forget the IDs and passwords and revert back to the old way of doing things: They write them down. This exposes an organization to potential compromise because these IDs and passwords can be easily obtained. Entitlement management provides a vehicle for organizations to define a single ID for a user across all business functions. Entitlement management also provides a way for organizations to productively guide the user through different functionalities of their business. This results in a productive user, and it reduces the time involved in maintaining multiple IDs. Statistics also show that if an organization does not manage user services effectively, they tend to lose potential customers to their competitors, resulting in reduced sales.

RECOVER

When describing core business systems, reliability and availability are not options; they are requirements fundamental to business survival.

When a disruption occurs, the organization's ability to quickly and cost-effectively recover and restore critical systems, processes, and data is vital. Organizations must be able to rapidly deploy their people, processes, and technology to recover business operations and information systems during a crisis because digital threats can appear from virtually nowhere and seriously compromise an unprepared organization even before the incident has been detected. Time, in this instance, truly is money because the losses in terms of downtime and damage to brand and corporate image can be significant. In spite of that, a recent survey showed that only 53 percent of organizations surveyed had business continuity programs in place.[8] An organization without a plan in place is an organization that is either unwilling to consider the realities of digital threats to corporate security or unwilling to allocate appropriate resources to address the issue, and either situation is unacceptable in today's globally-interconnected economy.

Business Continuity Planning

The security agenda's final item, business continuity planning, presents a forward-looking, enterprise-wide approach that takes into account both organizational and technical issues when identifying the processes that are critical to an organization's viability and success. Organizations with highly effective digital security programs in place have well-developed plans that include formal emergency response teams, regular and frequent reviews, and comprehensive testing and training.

All aspects of digital security must be taken into account when constructing a business continuity plan. As shown in Figure 5.7, the business continuity agenda item is a four-phase process that addresses six specific issues:

1. Having a roadmap to define needs proactively.
2. Being able to perform business impact assessments that take into account aligned business and security objectives.
3. Having tested and validated recovery strategies in place.

FIGURE 5.7 The Business Continuity Framework[9]

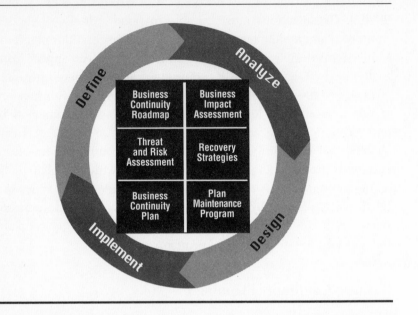

4. Ensuring that the plan in place is updated and reviewed continuously, and therefore always is ready for implementation.
5. Formalizing the plan and distributing it to critical personnel.
6. Being able to conduct threat and risk assessments from an enterprise-wide perspective.

The planning team involved in business continuity efforts follows management directives to craft policies that will guide the organization through the chaos caused by any disaster scenario, whether digital in nature or otherwise. Policies may address the impact of topics such as the number of senior executives that may travel together or be present at the same location, natural disasters, or a full-scale, coordinated denial-of-service attack that brings down an organizational web site. Risk assessments are conducted, governance methodologies are developed, and education programs are established to inform personnel at all levels. All communications are formalized and distributed to appropriate personnel for review and implementation. Resources are directed according to business requirements. Waivers are documented within an appropriate framework.

The architecture team must develop standards and guidelines that enable systems to maintain or regain full functionality as quickly as possible after a disaster scenario occurs. This may include building extraordinary redundancies into systems in different locations or into backup

---

A Business Continuity/Disaster Recovery Scenario

One week before Christmas, a truck backed into an electrical power pole in the shipping yard of a major distributor of groceries and supplies to restaurants, hospitals, nursing homes, and grocery stores. The cut power cable shorted out all communications into the distribution center and caused a small electrical fire in the computer room. Without the sophisticated order entry and shipping system, no orders could be shipped for the subsequent six days. At the peak period of sales for the year, this company could not deliver to its customers. Competitors quickly filled the gap and filled the delayed orders. The one-time loss of $15 million in sales was bad, but the long-term effects of departed customers weakened the company sufficiently to make it a takeover candidate in the following year. Within 15 months, the company had been sold and merged into a larger competitor.

Summary: The consequences of a single point of failure—a modest accident in a parking lot—caused the dissolution of a multi million-dollar company. A well-designed and exercised business continuity plan would have identified the potential point of failure, defined the impact of a failure of the computer systems, mitigated the risk, and developed plans to deal with the probability of occurrence. Sales would have been affected somewhat, but critical functions would have continued and major customers would have been satisfied. This example serves to underscore that business continuity plans are an obligation to the stakeholders of your organization: shareholders, employees, customers, suppliers, and regulators. Proactive companies are able to absorb the impact of catastrophic events and continue critical business processes to sustain their business. Unprepared companies suffer significant impacts to sales and market share.

arrangements, as well as other innovative, organization-specific security precautions. Business and technical requirements must be aligned and mapped, and technical designs of automated solutions developed. Any waivers should be analyzed to determine whether solutions exist or extensions to the technical security architecture need to be developed. RFPs are developed and published if technical remedies require third-party software or services.

The operations team must ensure that the developed standards and policies are deployed in repeated training and simulation exercises, and that those exercises are reviewed and updated as organizational changes take place. Monitoring personnel must conduct routine audits to ensure that compliance is maintained with both operational plans and logical systems. If the organization ever moves into disaster status, it is the monitoring personnel that will be key contributors to providing information in the initial and early stages of crisis management.

A highly effective digital security program will include all nine security agenda items, which together will enable an organization to mitigate risk, minimize vulnerabilities, and deflect threats; to coordinate appropriate, cost-effective responses to incidents when they occur; and to respond and recover smoothly and efficiently when the immediate attack has concluded. Having such a program requires that the executive-sponsored digital security team has open lines of communication up- and downstream within the organization, and receives acceptable levels of input from both business and technical groups. The digital security team must continually build the program, altering it as needed to maintain strategic internal and external alignments, and reflect new situations. Simulation exercises for attacks and responses must be conducted to determine organizational readiness and indicate areas in need of improvement. The executive management of an organization with an aligned, enterprise-wide, formalized, and validated digital security program that is proactive in outlook and continuously updated will attain a high level of confidence that the health of the organization will be maintained under the most extreme circumstances.

PART THREE
The Approach for Safety

The decision to be part of settling the American West had as much to do with possessing drive and ambition as it did with having diverse talents and skills. However, nothing beat experience when it came to clearing land, felling trees, building homes, or surviving blizzards, tornadoes, floods, and droughts. Knowing where to look for risks, knowing how to lessen the impact of crises when they occurred, and knowing what it would take to recover from those impacts were skills that could only be gained by experience. Seasoned veterans of the trail knew how to anticipate worst-case scenarios and develop responsive strategies. They knew how to implement those strategies when needed, adjust them according to the circumstance, and then, just as importantly, they knew when to begin moving forward.

Business organizations residing at the edge of the digital frontier have what it takes to remain there. After all, they had what it took to get there. However, the digital frontier is not a destination; it is part of a journey toward productivity and profitability. Organizations at its edge cannot indulge in the luxury of settling down and still expect to be secure. The digital frontier moves forward continuously. New hardware, updated software, and faster and simpler means of communication all bring new benefits as well as new risks. To harness digital technology is virtually impossible; therefore, to manage it is imperative.

In the nineteenth century, risk mitigation was simpler but no less important to the successful operation of a westward-bound wagon train. The trail captain determined the trip's timing with regard to the seasons, regional weather patterns, and terrain, and avoided the more treacherous territory when possible. Circling the wagons at night and posting lookouts were standard safety procedures, but it was still incumbent upon the members of the group to remain aware of their surroundings and report potential dangers.

Like America's early settlers, business organizations existing at the edge of the digital frontier must display constant alertness for signs that the situation is changing. There are understood risks that can be calculated, prepared for, deflected, and perhaps eliminated by applying the right methodology and utilizing the appropriate technology. However, there are still the unknown risks that arrive without warning. Storm clouds are a rare sight on the digital horizon; crises can develop literally at the speed of light. Although a company might have in place the most up-to-date firewalls and activity scanning countermeasures, the best authentication, authorization, and administration processes, and the most informed and well-trained personnel, it will still have vulnerabilities that have gone undetected.

This is why establishing a digital security culture within the organization is such a critical step to ensuring the success and viability of a digital security program. Being able to quantify risks, prioritize them, and communicate them is important. When the people in an organization understand the risks an organization faces, the remedies it must pursue, and the responses it must make, the digital security team will have less resistance to overcome as it begins to map risks and deploy counter-measures. A pervasive digital security culture will help to bring about a balance between highly effective security on one hand, and high productivity and growth on the other.

Part Three will provide a plan for accomplishing these important action items. Part Three explains why a digital security culture is important and offers recommendations for creating one. It explains why digital security is no longer merely a technical function, but a risk-management operation requiring executive sponsorship and executive involvement. A new approach to risk identification is presented, which focuses on controlling and containing threats, and mitigating those that are beyond reach. Part Three also offers a new perspective on risk that the traditional return-on-investment approach does not reflect. This new model of the secure organization is dependent on a fluid strategy built on reality-based scenarios.

6

The Security Culture

The differences between a digital security program and a world-class digital security program are twofold:

1. A highly effective program deploys all nine items on the security agenda and does so to the degree that they are fully aligned, enterprise-wide, continuous, proactive, validated, and formal.
2. A highly effective program is sponsored by the CEO and directed from the executive level.

The chapters in Part Two provided specific information on the first difference. This chapter provides details on the second.

It is absolutely vital that the executive who is the leader of the organization and the person who will charter a mandate for a highly effective digital security program understands the existing security environment within his or her organization. Unless the digital security program in place has attained wide-scale deployment, wholesale changes will have to occur to change the *security environment* into a *security culture*. The difference between these concepts is the difference between visiting someplace and living there, that is, between spending a few days seeing an ancient city's cathedrals and monuments, and spending a lifetime absorbing the sights, smells, sounds, and pace of that city.

Personnel within an organization that has a security environment know that there are procedures that must be followed and personal consequences if they are not. Personnel within an organization that has a security culture are aware of and follow the procedures. However, they also understand why those procedures are in place, and they understand not only the personal consequences of a security incident, but the effect a single incident can have on their business unit as well as the entire enterprise.

Building a security culture within an organization is unlike building a competitive edge in the marketplace. It cannot be done with rallies and pep talks, or with high-level meetings and occasional refresher courses. The parameters of the digital security program cannot be broadcast; if they are, anyone who's interested can determine where the vulnerabilities are. The security countermeasures deployed by the program must be applied and taught on a need-to-know basis. Everyone in the organization must learn basic logon procedures in order to be functional; everyone does not have to know what monitoring software is in place, where the surveillance cameras are, or that entrance to the executive-level floors requires biometric authorization. Therefore, the foundation of building a security culture is a strategic, carefully executed communication plan.

The first challenge to communicating the necessity for deploying a world-class digital security program may exist in the boardroom or executive suite. Myriad misperceptions about digital security exist at the highest levels of organizations, including:

- "Digital security is not our problem; it's an IT issue."
- "We have security in place (firewalls, etc.) to protect our networks. Why isn't that sufficient?"
- "Digital security will be a barrier to productivity."

- "We didn't have any problems last year. Why change what isn't broken?"
- "We can't afford it this year."

The rationales behind these misperceptions range from naïve to just plain wrong because:

- Digital security *is* an executive issue, and soon Congress may make it an even bigger one.
- Network security alone is not enough to keep out any determined hacker or malignant virus.
- A security event of sufficient magnitude will have a much more serious impact on productivity than security countermeasures ever will.
- Past performance is moot because threats change and new vulnerabilities appear every day.
- The only alternate to spending on security is spending on recovery.

THE CHIEF EXECUTIVE AS AN AGENT OF CHANGE

Change does not just happen in a large organization. It requires many hours of planning, execution, and maintenance. To effect change in an organization's security posture, the CEO must become the agent of change and set the digital security program's goals and priorities.

Instill a Heightened Sense of Awareness

It is imperative that a sense of urgency is established among executives and the board of directors to garner attention and support and facilitate cooperation and resource allocation. As the leader of this endeavor, it is incumbent upon the CEO to ensure that this sense of awareness and urgency permeates the organization and becomes woven into the fabric of the organization's culture. It must be sustained and nurtured so that it does not dissolve into complacency. This can be accomplished by launching a campaign across the enterprise and acknowledging interim successes on a periodic basis.

Build a Digital Security Guidance Council

There must always be one person driving any significant change in an organization, but that person cannot do it alone. A team—a digital security guidance council—must be assembled to continue the initiative and maintain its momentum. The digital security guidance council must have executive support and must include both executive and technical representation. Ideally, the digital security guidance council should comprise executives representing the following groups:

- Human resources
- Legal affairs
- Business operations areas (e.g., manufacturing or engineering)
- Internal audit
- Finance
- Information technology
- Risk management

The council must also have a defined hierarchy that breaks with tradition and elevates technical expertise to a senior level. The council members must have enough influence in the organization to effectively promote buy-in and instill change at all levels.

Establish a Timetable and Monitor Progress

When the digital security guidance council has determined what issues exist and the order in which the security agenda items should be deployed to resolve them, a schedule must be created. Reasonable deadlines should be developed, major milestones should be identified, and program goals should be clearly established. After the schedule has been crafted, project teams must be assembled and execution begun. It is difficult to create and sustain a high level of enthusiasm for a project that has as its goal the absence of an item or event. One goal of a digital security program is to enable an organization to contain and control a security incident, absorb the impact, and move forward. However, the ultimate goal of a digital security program is a smoothly running organization that successfully deflects digital attacks. It is a challenge, therefore, to define short-term successes: How and when does an organization decide to celebrate the lack of an attack? This conundrum, which is perhaps unique to security, serves to underscore the importance of identifying the milestones of program implementation.

A successful deployment of a global vulnerability management program or an on-time implementation of antivirus software across all desktops should be considered successful milestones, and they should be acknowledged as such. Short-term successes such as these can provide evidence that the sacrifices and efforts were worth it. They can also show to the skeptics and resisters that the program is working, and they may turn neutrals into supporters and reluctant supporters into active participants.

Roll Out an Enterprise-Wide Security Awareness and Training Program

Security goals should be communicated across the organization. Effective communication of the goals is essential if the digital security program is to be a success. The twin objectives of the communication program are as follows:

1. To ensure that all employees are aware of their roles and responsibilities on a routine day, as well as during a crisis.
2. To ensure that employees understand that the failure to perform a simple but vital security task could result in any number of security events, from unauthorized access to networks to the theft of critical information.

Every person in an organization, from the mailroom to the boardroom, must be indoctrinated to the security mindset. Therefore, the security awareness program must ensure that personnel at all levels:

- Understand the organization's digital security policies, standards, and guidelines and the employee responsibilities identified within those policies.
- Understand what constitutes a threat to digital assets.
- Are aware of the executive commitment to digital security, which includes seeing executives make the same changes in their behavior that they are requesting of the rest of the organization.
- Know who to contact with questions and concerns about digital security issues.

None of this "baked-in" security awareness will come about, however, if the communication is limited to passive means. There must be interactive training and communication. New procedures must be explained and demonstrated to reduce individuals' reluctance to implement security enhancements, and to reduce inevitable levels of frustration that follow any organizational change. For example, the addition of antivirus software that increases the time it takes to boot up a workstation, new logon procedures that require passwords to be changed on a routine basis, and the introduction of biometric devices or random password generators may inspire frustration and resistance among employees who are typically the late adopters, skeptics, or technophobes. Proper training and thorough communication can reduce or eliminate such concerns, which, if left unaddressed, could negate the efforts to enhance organizational security.

One fundamental objective of the security awareness and training program is to change employees' perspectives on digital security by communicating that digital security is important to the health of the organization. This change in perspective can lead to changes in behavior that will lead to a greater likelihood that employees' behavior will follow policy compliance expectations. As a means of initiating and continuing these changes, a training and awareness program could also include such measures as requiring new employees to read the policies and sign an acknowledgement that a certain level of understanding of both the policies and the consequences of violating them exists, and requiring annual renewal of that acknowledgement. It could involve the creation of an automated system that delivers policies to employees, and delivers tests that measure employees' understanding of digital security policies. It could continue with coordinated, periodic activities that communicate digital security issues to employees. Common methods to deliver these messages include sponsoring an organization-wide Security Awareness Week, distributing monthly e-mail newsletters, developing intranet sites, displaying security awareness posters, and holding security-related contests. Such a program could conclude with the digital security team making themselves available to employees to answer questions or refer questions to those who can answer them. The digital security team should maintain a level of visibility within the organization while disseminating the vision of the executive-sponsored digital security program.

Delivering the contents of the awareness program to employees is not unlike any other program implementation. It should be approached in a formal, consistent method that includes, but is not limited to, the following steps:

- Identify training scope and objectives.
- Identify trainees.
- Identify trainers.
- Gain management buy-in.
- Develop materials.
- Deliver content.
- Measure success.
- Assess, adjust, and repeat.

These steps should assist an organization's efforts to align its security culture to the security agenda. The success of the security agenda is dependent on this alignment because it is not just the expert who designs the intrusion detection system who is working toward security, but the administrative assistant who remembers to secure his or her workstation by checking for media left in the CPU and logging off the system before going to lunch, as well as the executive who adheres to the clear-desk policy before he or she leaves on a business trip.

Operating within a security culture implies a heightened awareness of the issues and the risks. In an organization that has created and now accepts the security culture, every person understands the risks and is aware enough to realize, for instance, that serial nuisances may be more than coincidental occurrences; they may be the start of an attack. The interplay of people, process, and technology has been identified earlier as one of the security drivers for an organization. The people variable is the most critical component of any digital security program. The commitment of an organization's personnel to the principles of security will determine the success or failure of the program.

7

The Risk Frontier

Recent world events have dramatically altered the concept of organizational risk. The hazards organizations face are potentially more dangerous than was previously thought. Threats appear more quickly and can turn into attacks without giving companies time to prepare effective defenses. Earlier chapters discussed agenda items for preparedness. In this chapter, we examine which agenda items to implement first, and why. Managing vulnerabilities is the responsibility of technical experts who have the full support of senior executives. Managing risk is the responsibility of senior executives.

It is the organization's executive management who must determine objectives, establish the organization's willingness to accept risk, and ascertain the organizational comfort level with regard to which risks to eliminate, which risks to mitigate, and which risks to accept. It is executive management who must achieve the objectives by investing in the right combination of the nine dimensions of the security agenda and ensuring that the highest level of security capability is achieved at the lowest possible cost.

MODELING AND DEFINING DIGITAL SECURITY RISK

In mid-October of 2001, President George W. Bush created the White House Office of Homeland Security by executive order with the mandate

FIGURE 7.1   Threat Categories

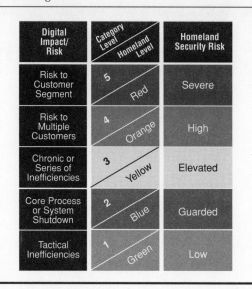

to assess America's preparedness to deal with terrorist attacks and to coordinate the detection, deterrence, protection, response and recovery, and incident management of any future attacks. The Director of Homeland Security created a hierarchy for assessing threats to the United States and its citizens and interests.

The rightmost column in Figure 7.1 lists the threat categories developed by the department: low, guarded, elevated, high, and severe. These threat categories apply as easily to individual organizations managing digital security as they do to the nation. For that reason, they can easily be adapted to describe the digital security risks faced by companies, as shown in the columns to the left and in the middle of the diagram.

A severe threat (category 5) to an organization is one that would result in a significant risk to a customer segment; this is a threat that an organization will spend significant resources to deflect, and one for which there is no short-term fix. An example of such a threat is the public release of sensitive or private customer information, which would destroy the credibility of the brand image. A high threat (category 4) is

Homeland Security Advisory System

Low: A low risk of terrorist attacks is present. Suggested defensive activities include refining and conducting preplanned exercises, training personnel, and assessing and mitigating vulnerabilities.

Guarded: There is a general risk of terrorist attacks. Suggested activities include ensuring emergency communications systems are in place and functional.

Elevated: A significant risk of terrorist attacks exists. Suggested activities include increasing surveillance at critical facilities and assessing threat-specific protocols.

High: A high risk of terrorist attacks exists. Suggested protective measures include coordinating security efforts with appropriate authorities and preparing to work under extraordinary conditions, such as with a dispersed workforce.

Severe: This is the highest state of alert, and suggested   security precautions include pre-positioning response personnel and redirecting other personnel to address potential needs.

http://www.whitehouse.gov/news/releases/
2002/03/20020312.html

one that would present a significant risk to multiple customers. An elevated risk (category 3) represents an event that is the result of chronic or serial inefficiencies, which would impact market share and public and/or employee confidence. An example of a category 3 risk is a web site that is continually breaking down or coming under attack. A guarded risk (category 2) describes incidents that involve the shutdown of core processes or systems, such as e-mail. Low-risk incidents (category 1) include events that could be described as nuisances or tactical inefficiencies when taken alone.

Figure 7.2 is the graphic representation of these levels of threat intensity considered in the context of the frequency of occurrence and the level of impact on the organization. The curved line is the organization's *risk posture*, which is the level of organizational security as aligned

---

FIGURE 7.2   The Security Risk Framework

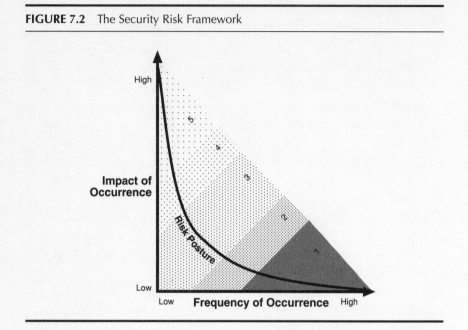

with the threat categories described above. It is the line that signifies the theoretical capabilities of the organization to mitigate risk (up and to the right of the curve) and the theoretical risk that an organization is accepting (down and to the left) by choosing to take the chance that those incidents will not occur or have impacts that are within the limits of tolerance. The shading denotes various types and levels of incidents that an organization may experience.

It should be noted that the scale of categories described above is entirely relative to both the organization and the specific situation it is facing. For example, a hacking event that brings down a web site is certainly a security incident, although the severity of it would depend on the organization's usage and reliance on that web site for core business. In addition, a category 1 or 2 threat combined with other category 1 or 2 incidents within a compressed time frame could cause the threat level to escalate rapidly, and even a category 1 or 2 threat can become a category 4 or 5 as the result of media attention. It bears mentioning that repeated category 1 threats that do not escalate still consume organizational resources that otherwise would and should be used to manage higher-level threats.

However, it must be said that an employee harvesting and selling sensitive or critical information in small increments over a long period of time is also considered a security incident for this discussion, as are the small but incremental attacks of a hacker taking a "low and slow" approach. There is a range of sophistication associated with malicious hackers. The range spans from a "script kiddie" (a hacker with limited technical knowledge and ability) with a goal of publicity to a highly skilled person whose motives lie in deception and theft with the goal of monetary gain. Although the impact that some script kiddies inflict on organizations cannot be ignored, those incidents represent category 1, 2, or perhaps 3 hacking events.

Scenario: A Low and Slow Attack

When prowling around an organization's digital assets, script kiddies usually leave wakes of destruction much like the proverbial bull in a china shop. The category 4 and 5 hacking events are caused by highly skilled hackers that prowl through and pillage digital assets with a low and slow mentality. "Low and slow" describes hackers who are careful to not trip alarms, trigger detection systems, or let their surreptitious activities be logged. They operate by stealth, gaining access to a system under the radar like military maneuvers in which planes fly low and slowly to avoid detection by the enemy.

The nature of these attacks makes it likely that these low and slow hackers negatively impact organizations on a much larger scale than realized. Organizations without a digital security program in place are unable to detect any of their activities most of the time. The activities that are detected will appear to be uncorrelated and, therefore, will be classified as category 1 events; they appear to be little more than nuisances that require little or no attention.

P@tchM4n, an experienced hacker known for his finesse in finding and exploiting system vulnerabilities, recently conducted an attack on a large financial institution that resulted in a continuous leak of thousands of private customer records over several months. He conducted a quiet scan of the organization's external-facing network, essentially "casing the joint" as he looked for vulnerabilities.

After finding what he was looking for—a known vulnerability ineffectively patched—he commenced his operations. After gaining administrator access to the server, he skillfully installed a root kit, which is essentially a back door to the system, and tools to assist with further unauthorized access. Using this system as a launch pad, P@tchM4n was able to penetrate the internal network and gain access to servers that support the customer and financial systems. Up to this point, he had taken extreme pains to avoid tripping security countermeasures, including limiting himself to a few select activities each day or each week. Once the target financial systems were found, they, too, were scanned low and slow for vulnerabilities.

He didn't find any, but that didn't bother him. Nor did it stop him. He just set some interim goals and started snooping through files on the system. Fortunately for him, some users, including senior management, had placed their system IDs and passwords into text files, which are unprotected and could be opened by a moderately skillful script kiddie.

Over the next few months, P@tchM4n repeatedly gained access to a database containing customer names, addresses, birth dates, credit card numbers, and Social Security numbers: a veritable buffet of private information, including detailed data on spending habits. P@tchM4n quietly extracted this information and, without too much trouble, located a buyer willing to pay an exorbitant price for this easily resalable information that fits in a shirt pocket.

P@tchM4n's activity was never discovered while he was engaged in it, and his fun came to an abrupt end after only six months when the network was upgraded. The original system on the network perimeter that he had compromised, and on which he had installed the root kit, incurred a hardware failure. The failed system was replaced with another that didn't have a root kit on it, didn't have the hacker's unauthorized but seemingly legitimate ID, and had been patched for the vulnerability that had been exploited. The ironic result of the system failure was that a hacker's window into the company network was closed.

Summary: Incidents like this one create the potential for huge impacts in the area of category 4 and 5 events. Not only was the institution's privacy compromised, but its customers' privacy was compromised even more severely. The fact that the activity had been going on for six months without being noticed, and probably would have continued, is sobering. This trusted system had been severely compromised and the organization was unaware of the compromise. Although this incident did not become public knowledge, it could have and might still by a variety of means, any one of which could be embarrassing or worse to the financial institution. The customer list should appear somewhere in its entirely with information identifying its origins. It could be recovered as part of a criminal investigation.

Implementing a highly effective digital security program would drastically improve not only an organization's ability to detect this kind of hacker activity, but also to increase the chances of preventing this from occurring elsewhere. A vulnerability management program would help to preclude compromised servers. Strong monitoring capabilities that continuously review server access logs and audit systems for compliance to policies, standards, and guidelines would help identify unauthorized access and identify the presence of IDs and passwords in widely readable files.

Low and Slow Scenario: Lessons to Be Learned

This scenario serves to highlight a critical point that cannot be overemphasized: near-crisis events occur with startling frequency. Many are successfully detected and deflected, and an additional percentage are effectively contained. This should not, however, be viewed as a triumph. It should be viewed instead as evidence in support of the many dire statistics that indicate increasing rates of successful attack or penetration.

Therefore, the executive management team must determine which threats it faces and what the impact of those threats would be should they occur, disregarding for the moment the probability of those threats occurring. Once executives understand the threats, they also must determine the level of organizational security with which they are comfortable. They must also determine the real level at which the business objectives of productivity and profitability are balanced by security measures, which means understanding that productivity and profitability may be irrevocably compromised if an unlikely or improbable category 5 event occurs but has not been anticipated. The next steps are determining the desired security end-state for the organization, and then determining the mix of fully deployed security agenda items that will enable the organization to reach that state. Using this top-down approach to address threats will likely require significant systemic changes to the organization, which is why such changes require executive-level involvement and sponsorship.

This approach is controversial because the typical approach to digital security takes a bottom-up approach by addressing frequently occurring risks, for instance category 1 threats, before moving to less probable, higher-impact threats. The reason that approach does not work with high-impact threats is that executive management requires the digital security team to provide a traditional return-on-investment model to justify the deployment of resources toward mitigating high-impact, low-probability threats. Unable to develop and deliver that model or a message that stresses the strategic nature of managing high-impact risk, the digital security team may fail to persuade management to deploy the appropriate resources. This can leave the management with the mistaken impression that the organization is doing everything it can that has a measurable return on investment to manage risk. However, if management does not understand that they have to make some alterations that may not have a justifiable return on investment, the digital security team may be left with the impression that management doesn't support an enhanced digital security program since it won't provide the necessary resources. Therefore, the result of taking the traditional, return-on-investment-based approach is an organization in which digital security operates on an IT level and not an enterprise level. The enterprise view of risk contravenes tradition by focusing on developing capabilities to mitigate the impact of a category 4 or 5 threat (rather than focusing on the probability of occurrence) and taking steps to mitigate that impact to the degree possible as quickly as is feasible to maintain clear alignment to business objectives.

The next step in this new model of the enterprise view of risk is the most important: determining what constitutes a category 4 or 5 risk to an organization. Understanding this enables executives to deploy resources effectively. Specific risks are discussed later in this chapter; however, the foundation of understanding and addressing those risks is determining *the point at which control and containment of the incident become critical to the future of the organization.* Movement past this point may escalate the situation beyond the control of the digital security team.

It is imperative that executive management and the digital security team know what can drive an organization to the point at which the ability to control and contain an event is lost. Knowing where that point of control is for an organization is the key to containing a security event. As has been stated, any event, even a category 1 event, can spiral out of control for any number of reasons. As the damage gains momentum, it will move the event beyond that *fulcrum of control* and virtually nothing can be done to stop the event from materially damaging the marketability, the profitability, or even the viability of the business.

As shown in Figure 7.3, events that are determined to be above the fulcrum of control are events that executive management must approach

FIGURE 7.3   The Risk Frontier

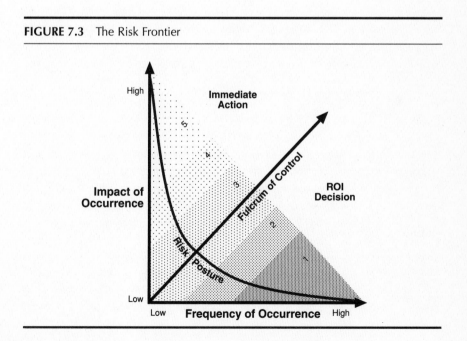

from an enterprise perspective. If it has been determined that a certain event, the loss of a mission-critical web site, for instance, would be a category 5 event, then mitigation strategies cannot be created using a traditional return-on-investment approach. Mitigating that risk must begin immediately, with the understanding that business continuity will be the only return on investment.

The goal for incidents above the line is prevention or mitigation of incidents that cause material damage, for example business continuity issues, whereas the goal for incidents below the line is preventing the escalation of incidents beyond the fulcrum of control, for example, intrusion detection and incident response issues. The prevention and mitigation strategies are accomplished by having in place the appropriate combination of agenda items and mature PAOM capabilities. Implementing the nine agenda times and deploying the PAOM framework will create a systematically less risky environment, which will effectively move the organizational risk posture toward the intersection of the axis, which represents the lowest possible impact of occurrence and lowest possible frequency of occurrence. This movement represents achieving a state in which risk is managed to the appropriate tolerance level of the organization, its shareholders, and employees.

Scenario: A High-Impact Risk Proactively Mitigated

A manufacturing organization relies on a handful of integrated applications running on hundreds of systems that provide information and services to production fabrication sites across the world. The systems that support these applications physically reside in a single data center. After recognizing the potential impact of a disaster to this data center, the company conducted a business impact analysis to identify the exact processes that would be affected by such an incident, including the various thresholds of loss associated with extended outages. The analysis revealed that more than five days of outages for these applications would significantly impact the marketability, viability, or profitability of the business. Analysis of the current disaster recovery capabilities of the organization revealed that it would take fifteen days to bring the applications back online and make them available to the fabrication sites.

The executive management realized the firm was carrying an unacceptable amount of risk should the data center be destroyed in a disaster. To mitigate this risk, the company decided to focus its attention on two areas: improving its disaster recovery capabilities, and implementing high-availability solutions to reduce the duration of a possible outage. Of the many solutions that could be deemed high-availability, management chose to deploy technology that provided instantaneous replication of all application data to another data center where "warm", or waiting, systems were on standby in case they were needed. In the event of a disaster at the main data center, the warm systems could be brought live and the data, having been continuously replicated from the main data center, would be ready and available to employees and customers. Bringing this warm data center to a live status could be accomplished within twelve hours, leaving the company in a position to maintain marketability, viability, and profitability despite having suffered a major disaster. Essentially, this company addressed a category 4 or 5 incident by deploying resources that would enable it to contain and control the situation should it present itself. Arguably, the executive management team's proactive approach turned a category 4 or 5 event into an event that could be classified as a category 2 or 3 event. The company's curve, its risk posture, has been moved down and to the left (Figure 7.3). Its risk is being managed.

High-Impact Risk Scenario: Lessons to Be Learned

The impact of similar digital security incidents will have different outcomes in various organizations depending on an organization's ability to control and contain the incident. The ability to control and contain is directly related to the ultimate category that is assigned to the incident. Recall that, by default, executive management must act to immediately mitigate risks for some category 3s, all category 4s, and all category 5s. Further recall that multiple category 1s or 2s that occur within a short amount of time should actually be categorized as category 3s or higher. This reclassification to a higher category level is all based on the ability to control and contain a digital security situation. The much-publicized Code Red and Code Red II worms bring to light two scenarios that highlight how category escalation can happen and bring about critical impacts to business due to the inability of a digital security program to contain and control incidents.

Scenario: An Attack That Was Contained and Controlled

Code Red II infected the internal and perimeter network of a large professional services firm, impairing some internal network traffic and crippling the ability to communicate digitally with the outside world. This included its own consultants working at client sites, who were unable to access digital resources on the company's network. The executives at the company brought in some of their own experts to respond to the situation.

Over the next 36 hours, a series of decisions were made with the support of executive management. The decisions led to a near-full recovery of internal network availability and a recovery of the ability to communicate digitally with the outside world. Many difficult but critical decisions were made in the early phases of the response, particularly a decision to shut down all computers that communicate with the outside world. As difficult as this decision was, the company's digital security experts were able to gain executive buy-in that it was necessary to isolate the incident, control and contain the damage, and enable a quick recovery. Within 36 hours, recovery had been accomplished and there was a full resumption of service availability. This rapid and thorough recovery enabled critical timekeeping and accounting services to process consultant hours, leading to invoice generation and payment processing, and avoiding the loss of potentially millions of dollars of revenue in the form of lost interest.

Summary: This scenario represents a category 1 or 2 event that had the real potential of moving to a 3 or 4, but with an effective, executive-sponsored digital security program in place the incident was controlled and contained, and did not exceed a category 2.

Scenario: An Attack That Escalated Beyond Containment and Control

Code Red II infected the internal and perimeter network of a large telecommunications company, impairing internal network traffic, crippling the ability to communicate digitally with the outside world, and effectively bringing customer services to a halt. The personnel at the company were unable to isolate the incident. Furthermore, they were unable to recognize the extent to which the virus had penetrated their environment. Once they did realize the extent of penetration, it was too late to take actions to control and contain the incident.

Having lost the ability to control and contain, the impact of the event intensified over the next 48 hours. This led to lost market share, broken service-level agreements, and lost revenue that severely affected the company's ability to compete and win back customers. Unfortunately, soon after this incident occurred, market conditions took a turn for the worse, making it impossible for the company to redeem its lost market share or recover from lost revenues.

Although the initial event is the same as in the first scenario, the nature of the businesses changes the intensity of the threat. To a telecommunications firm, this second scenario represents a category 2 or 3 event. However, because it was neither controlled nor contained, it quickly escalated to the level of a category 4 or 5 event that, when compounded by economic conditions that may not have been foreseeable, eventually sped the company's loss of a large segment of its business.

Containment and Control Scenarios: Lessons to Be Learned

As these two real-world scenarios point out, although category 4 and 5 events are by definition catastrophic, their impact on an organization can be lessened. These scenarios emphasize the point that an organization can only control and contain the situation if it takes a proactive approach and has fortified itself against attack by employing preemptive countermeasures such as intrusion detection and incident response programs.

If an organization is not proactive about avoiding attacks, its risk posture remains too far to the right of the axis (Figure 7.3). Occupying this position means the organization may not recover from a category 4 or 5 event because no precautions have been taken. Organizations move their curve down and to the left by investing in the nine security agenda items and developing the organizational capabilities detailed in Chapter 4.

Deploying and maintaining a highly effective digital security program will push the organization's risk posture toward the intersection of the axes (low impact/low frequency). However, advancing technology will provide a counterbalancing pull away from the intersection and toward the edge of the digital frontier, which is defined in part by continual technological growth that is marked unfortunately by both beneficial and destructive attributes, and the adoption, usage, and reliance on those technologies. If an organization's prevention and mitigation efforts are not formal, proactive, and continuous and if they are not aligned to business objectives, deployed enterprise-wide, and validated to rigorous standards, then the organization's risk posture will move away from the axis by default as advances in technology intensify the risks.

APPROACHING RISK MANAGEMENT

As we just stated, digital security teams focus by default on the lower threat category incidents, and with the nine agenda items in place and fully implemented, that is more easily done. It is up to senior management to identify the most significant threats to the organization and its business objectives, and deploy resources to manage them, with the focus on prevention.

Defining what constitutes a category 4 or 5 threat to an organization is an exercise in relativity, and that is why it is a task for executive management. No one else in an organization has or should have such detailed knowledge of the organization, its risks, and its capabilities for protecting itself from those risks. For example, to an exclusively online entity such as eBay or Amazon, a service outage to an external web site would be at category 3 or 4, or possibly even a category 5, security incident. The same incident occurring on a non-revenue-generating web site for a major oil company, for example, might constitute a category 2 event. However, a service outage to an internal web site that provides critical supply-chain functionality might rate a category 3 or 4 designation to an Exxon or a Mobil, but may not even be applicable to an organization like eBay. Therefore, the process for determining what the category 3, 4, and 5 events are for an organization is described as follows:

- High-value digital assets must be identified and ranked.
- Threats to and vulnerabilities within those assets must be determined.
- An impact analysis must be performed.

Armed with the outcomes of this process, executive management should be prepared to set the bar for preventing and mitigating the threats by deploying adequate resources. The executive management team has to take the time to work through potential crisis scenarios. Efficient, adequate deployment of financial, technological, and personnel resources may not, and probably will not, fit the classic return-on-investment scenario that most business enterprises have traditionally used. The decision to deploy resources to address high-level risks cannot be a superficial, bandage-type approach. Executive management must understand and communicate to peers and board members that appropriate resource allocation is a proactive measure that will not only reflect but build an enterprise-wide organizational commitment, that such an allocation is justified because of the alignment between business goals and security objectives, and that if it is to fulfill its preset goal of establishing world-class digital security, it must be endorsed at all levels by senior management.

8

Road Map for Success

Identifying threats, putting countermeasures in place to avoid them, and taking steps to lessen the harm they may produce are important procedures to follow before setting out on any journey, and these procedures must be updated en route. America's pioneers took months to prepare for their momentous trips across unnamed, untamed territory. When they set out to reshape the existing frontier, they had to prepare for any and every eventuality, as well as for possibilities they couldn't imagine. It took planning and flexibility, experience and creativity to withstand a disaster, absorb the impact, and finish the journey.

Life at the digital frontier is much the same. Leading a business organization to the edge of that frontier takes just as much planning, creativity, strength, and experience as required by the early settlers to meet and overcome known and unknown challenges and still survive. But it's not just survival. When an organization has been stricken by disaster, whether malicious hacking has brought down networks and compromised information or a physical crisis has affected critical infrastructure, an organization must respond appropriately and initiate its planned recovery procedures immediately, perhaps even before the crisis has reached its conclusion.

To be effective, this set of plans must be understood by everyone in the organization, not just those at the executive level. The plans must be disseminated, and the procedures must be practiced. All the careful planning and detailed documentation in the world cannot prevent the burst of adrenaline that happens the moment a crisis strikes. However, what happens as that adrenaline begins to dissipate is the true measure of how close an organization is to having a world-class security structure in place. When a crisis occurs within an organization that has instituted and nurtured a security culture, procedures are already underway as the adrenaline rush begins to fade. Emergency response countermeasures are implemented in the midst of chaos, and recovery plans move things forward at a sure, reasoned pace while other organizations have either become suspended in disbelief or are reacting with panic, rushing about in ineffectual circles. In a crisis situation, having a plan and executing it is not just good business sense, it is quickly becoming the fiduciary responsibility of many executive managers.

The idea of digital security, specifically business continuity, is not new. Such plans have been detailed and documented by organizations for years. However, there has never been a time in our nation's history when the vulnerability of business operations been so universally recognized. The events of September 11, 2001, brought that vulnerability into the executive orbit of regard with stark clarity. In the face of such events, the need for digital security procedures assumes a much more prominent role in organizations for which digital technology is the means of their functionality. Organizations today need a map for successful development and implementation of such procedures, and a proven plan for restructuring an organization to ensure enterprise-wide understanding of the importance of digital security and of fostering a security culture.

POSITIONING THE ORGANIZATION WITHIN THE INDUSTRY

Earlier chapters have detailed the reasons why executive leadership, sponsorship, and direction are critical to the success of a digital security program. What must be underscored, however, is that the CEO doesn't have to understand the technologies as long as he or she understands the risks associated with their implementation and has the ability to balance effectively the organization's productivity needs and digital security risks.

Because companies continue to invest in technology for productivity gains and competitive advantage, the edge of the digital frontier is a highly dynamic state of existence and companies at that edge cannot afford to view security as a static end-state. It isn't, and it can't be. The increasing use of and reliance on technology continually pushes the edge of the digital frontier outward, increasing the probability and impact of security incidents. Organizations that want to remain at the edge of the digital frontier must ensure their risk management strategies include heightened security awareness and fully deployed counter-measures. This inclusive focus on digital security issues will exert an equal and opposite push to lessen the impact and reduce the probability of security incidents while organizations continue to adopt new technologies that enhance their core business.

Pushing back the curve in Figure 8.1 (down and to the left) requires that companies know what their current risk posture is, and what they

FIGURE 8.1   Forces in Motion at the Digital Frontier

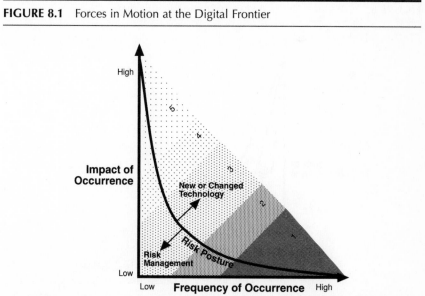

want it to be. Only then can the decision to move the curve be made. Although moving toward the intersection of the axes for the safety and welfare of the company is the ultimate goal, the first goal must be to move the curve to a position inside the curve of industry peers, as shown in Figure 8.2.[1] Positioning the organization relative to the competition is important because if a security incident of a critical magnitude occurred and affected an entire industry (for example, if a security breach within one of the major commodity exchanges brought trading to a halt for a period of time), some organizations will absorb the impact and move on. Others that may not have an effective digital security program in place will falter.

The potential competitive advantage of having a highly effective digital security program in place cannot be ignored. If only a few firms are able to sustain and absorb an impact that debilitates the rest of their industry, several critical lessons will be learned by the public, as well as by shareholders and employees of those companies and their competi-

FIGURE 8.2 The Ideal Relative Position for an Organization

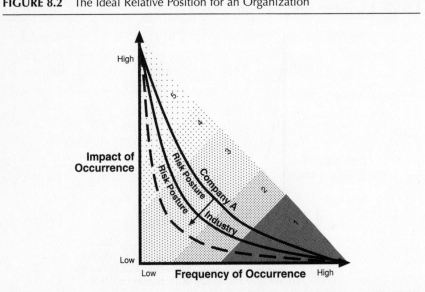

tors. The most important lesson, and the one the market will remember, is that only those few were able to contain and control the damage. Only those few realized that digital security is strategic to the success of the business and took the necessary step of implementing an effective program. Another important lesson, which the market will also remember, is that the other firms in the industry considered digital security non-essential. That sort of perception by the marketplace can be the competition's greatest exploitable vulnerability in terms of both digital security and market share.

Executives who are thought of as leaders in their companies and in their industries already have digital security within their orbit of regard, and are working to push back the risk posture curve to a point beyond industry standards. Every company can effect this change if the CEO is willing to:

- Set the objectives for digital security, ensuring that they align with and support business objectives.
- Allocate resources for a program to achieve and maintain digital security, including monitoring and measuring the program itself.
- Promote an enterprise-wide digital security culture.
- Reduce the total risk of security failures while eliminating high-impact events.
- Conceive a charter for the digital security program that establishes goals and standards for an implementation framework.

When the nine items of the security agenda have been implemented and display all six characteristics of a world-class digital security program, when the organization's fulcrum of control has been identified, and when the digital security spending gap that has been allowed to exist has been reduced, an organization's risk posture curve will begin to move.

RESOURCE ALLOCATION

Every company spends something on digital security. Many executives think they spend enough. The reality is that few actually do spend enough. The biggest problem with determining how much to spend is not only understanding which programs and countermeasures to implement, but why they're necessary. The answer to that problem is that the correct amount to spend is however much is needed to position the organization properly on the risk posture curve *and maintain control of that placement* to enable the organization to absorb the impact of a significant security event and move forward.

We live in a new world and we face new risks, and resource allocation criteria must acknowledge those facts. Traditional budgeting approaches don't work when the subject is digital security because:

- *The amount of money spent doesn't guarantee a certain level of security will be achieved.* It is the mix that matters: the organization, its current security profile, its desired security profile, and the effectiveness of the fully deployed nine security agenda items.
- *There is not a fixed correlation between investment and return.* The best possible return is invisible: an organization that runs smoothly and suffers little if any damage from a digital security incident.
- *The security purchase isn't about image.* It's not branded. In fact, a comprehensive digital security program is probably something an organization would not want to publicize, reducing the temptation for hackers to consider it a challenge.

The amount of money an organization should spend on security is relative to its situation. The only rule is not to spend more than the potential loss due to a security failure. Executive management has to set the parameters of the digital security program by determining the organization's strengths and weaknesses (e.g., people, process, technology, or infrastructure) and by prioritizing risks to determine which require immediate action and which can be addressed in a less critical time frame (e.g., physical infrastructure, privacy issues, corporate espionage, fiduciary responsibilities, or mitigating future risk by building digital security into plans for expansion). When the parameters have been set, the executive management team can task the digital security team with building the most cost-effective system to those specifications.

Even within the same industry, organizations face different risks. Every company has unique needs and capabilities because each has its own competitive position in the marketplace. The decision to allocate resources for digital security cannot rest simply on how much a program is going to cost, or how much the competition is spending. *The amount the competition is spending doesn't come into the equation; what the competition's money is doing to their risk posture does.* One of the reasons these issues do not come into play is that each organization has its own set of core customers and suppliers, each of whom has conditions of their own that have to be considered when the CEO is viewing the enterprise as a whole. One organization may be able to implement an intrusion detection system within three months, for X amount of dollars, and the system requires five dedicated staff members to operate and maintain. An established industry competitor implementing the same agenda item may spend more or less time and money, and require more or fewer people to run it.

The reasons for the sometimes large differences in implementation and execution costs can vary significantly. Perhaps the first company deployed a system that focused on a medium- to high-impact network perimeter because that firm's network perimeter contains a handful of servers, applications, and other digital hardware. The second company's network perimeter may contain dozens of servers, applications, and other hardware. The first company may have built expansion capabilities into the system when it was designed, whereas the second company had to take its dense network configuration and retrofit it to include state-of-the-art intrusion detection capabilities. These and many other variables can and will impact timing and resources in this simple scenario, but the point is that implementing effective intrusion detection in the two firms will require significantly different levels of effort and spending. This cost/benefit issue goes to the heart of digital security: Is it "baked in" or "painted on"?

INSURING AGAINST DIGITAL SECURITY EVENTS

There is a small but growing trend for firms to attempt to insure their way out of digital security risks. There is one serious flaw in this approach: There is no insurance policy that can substitute for having in place a comprehensive, enterprise-wide digital security program. Why? Some of the reasons are as follows:

- Buying an insurance policy changes the impact of an event; it does not change the probability of occurrence.
- There is no blanket insurance for security events; no organization can be insured against everything. Only certain events or occurrences can be covered and, as the business world learned in the autumn of 2001, if you can't imagine it, you can't protect yourself against it.
- Even when the potential for events can be identified, an organization must know its probability of risk for that event and the probable extent of damage in order to know how much insurance to buy. If there has been no risk assessment conducted, there is no way of knowing these things.
- Not having identified risk or attempted to mitigate it and not having the ability to investigate an incident would make it significantly more difficult for an organization to support an insurance claim sufficiently to meet the criteria for insurance settlement.
- If a settlement can be reached, collecting on an insurance claim after a serious security breach will not restore consumer or shareholder confidence. The questions of why and how the event happened in the first place will still be left unanswered.

Although these are valid reasons why insurance cannot replace a security program, this is not to say that insurance has no place in a comprehensive digital security program. It is *after* a comprehensive digital security program is in place that insurance becomes a cost-effective enhancement. The risks have been identified. Some have been mitigated and perhaps some have been made negligible. Proactive countermeasures have been deployed. Personnel have been educated to the risks and ramifications of security incidents. At this point, the executive management team has assessed the organization's strengths and weaknesses; it knows what assets it wants to insure, and what events it wants to insure against. It may still be a challenge to determine how much insurance the organization might need or what it might cost to clean up after a disaster. However, those decisions can be reached from a position of strength based on knowledge rather than weakness based on fear.

TABLE-TOP EXERCISES

Though many organizations conduct situational analyses, in 1996 New York Mayor Rudolph Giuliani created the Office of Emergency Management (OEM) by executive order. The OEM reset the standard for coordinated, multiagency emergency response, and Giuliani's approach brought about an evolution in "what-if" role-playing exercises, which he called table-top exercises. Key administrative and technical members of strategic city departments were required to participate in disaster scenarios of many descriptions and magnitudes. Participants were not informed beforehand of which scenarios would be conducted in order to make the exercises and the responses as realistic as possible, and so the Mayor could gauge the participants' ability to think on their feet.

Different scenarios focused on how to respond effectively to the immediate situation, whether a natural or man-made disaster, as well as on addressing the myriad critical issues faced by a city inhabited by millions of people: public safety, sanitation, transportation, and others. The corresponding needs were prioritized, and the objective of establishing order was aligned with the objective of keeping the rest of New York City's agencies secure and functional. The scenarios and responses were monitored and tested, reassessed and redesigned, then executed again. It was only because of this formal, proactive, administration-wide training and education program that emergency management personnel were able to respond as quickly and effectively as they did when the unthinkable happened on September 11, 2001.

There is no reason that an organization cannot apply the same principles and practices to ensure its recovery and continuity after enduring a disaster. Crises of all types—individual and compounded digital events, as well as hybrid digital-physical incidents—should be simulated then reviewed in an ongoing cycle. Table-top exercises and their organizational equivalent serve to heighten awareness of the probability and magnitude of category 4 or 5 events, and to underscore the importance of knowing what must be done in a crisis, why, and in what sequence. Such exercises are necessary to ensure the full acceptance of a security culture within an organization and to ensure to the degree possible that disaster recovery and business continuity plans will be effective if they are ever actually deployed. Such exercises are role-playing scenarios on a grand scale that can validate an organization's plans by assessing the assignment of roles and responsibilities, and the actions taken by the executives and senior managers who would be key figures in a disaster situation.

The scenarios are event-driven; the response to a web site defacement, no matter how severe, will not be the same as to a major communications hub for the organization being penetrated and pilfered, or to a private communications satellite's signal being jammed. The ability of those who will be central figures in any scenario to respond appropriately and effectively should be tested. If there is to be any chance of the organization absorbing the impact and sustaining the business after an event, insiders have to understand the risks, the ramifications of their actions, and the potential for unforeseen consequences, as well as the various permutations that can mark an incident. If the risks are unknown, there is no way to plan a response. Panic and chaos are not characteristics associated with successful emergency response procedures, although they frequently seem to be the most widely relied upon. The role of the CEO in the table-top exercises is to identify digital security goals before any plans can be devised or executed. Is the goal functionality within X hours after a category 4 or 5 event? The CEO may have to ignore the boxes on the organizational chart when determining who is best suited to direct the recovery effort for each scenario. These issues are difficult to address, as are the many other questions that will have to be asked and answered before disaster recovery and business continuity plans can be made. However, they must be asked and answered if the digital security program that has been painstakingly developed and deployed is to serve its ultimate function: defending the organization at the digital frontier.

THE ORBIT OF REGARD

When a digital security event can impact an organization's bottom line and maybe even its ability to continue as a business, the CEO must set the security agenda for the organization, and all of the agenda items presented in earlier chapters must come into his or her orbit of regard. When viewed from the perspective of survival rather than return on investment, digital security is as critical to the organization as are its products, services, and market share. It is strategically important.

As shown in Figure 8.3, there are several core concerns that have traditionally remained within the scope of executive management: market share, brand image, customer service, growth, and productivity. With the advent of the digital age, another topic came into view: information security. In the 1980s, when few people were using computers, and many companies were only beginning to explore how to use them to enhance performance, security was not an issue other than in the physical sense. The machines and the buildings that housed them had to be protected. The 1990s brought an explosion of advances in technology and by the end of that decade, even children were online and computer literate. But in the fervor of growth and productivity increases, security was still largely overlooked despite the development of a disturbing and growing trend of malicious, computer-related events directed at large corporations. The events of September 11, 2001, served to finally bring the entire concept of digital security onto the radar screen of executive concerns.

Now, digital security affects nearly every aspect of an organization's life and culture. When critical systems go down, whether physically or logically, everything relying on them or connected to them stops. If private or sensitive information is released on the Internet, it can be copied

FIGURE 8.3   The CEO's Orbit of Regard

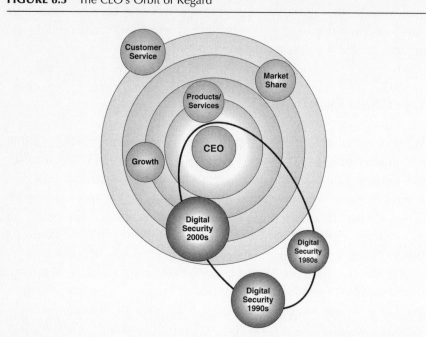

and stored by millions of users; it may be out there forever. If an incident affects a large segment of the public and the media focus their attention on it, the corporate image may suffer.

It is up to the CEO to ensure that a digital security culture not only pervades the organization, but exerts an influence on every aspect of it. Security awareness must be the gravitational force that keeps everything else—market share, brand, customer service, productivity, and growth—in perpetual motion at the edge of the digital frontier.

APPENDIX A

Security-Related Laws and Regulations

U.S. LAWS

The USA Patriot Act of 2001

This law gave extensive new powers to both domestic law enforcement and international intelligence agencies with respect to monitoring digital and/or electronic communications and transmissions. It also eliminated the checks and balances that previously gave courts the opportunity to ensure that these powers were not abused by agencies as they had been in years past. Some examples of the new law follows:

- The government can now observe what search terms Internet users are putting into search engines and which web sites they have visited.
- Internet service providers are required to provide law enforcement and intelligence agencies private user information upon request.
- U.S. intelligence agencies are authorized to use nationwide roving wiretaps.

- Businesses can now be required to provide an individual's educational, medical, financial, mental health, and travel records of which they are the custodians. For more information, see http://www.epic.org/privacy/terrorism/hr3162.html.

Impact: privacy, incident response, policies, standards, and guidelines.

The Digital Privacy Act of 2000

This law amended previous government surveillance laws with respect to electronic information, such as e-mail addresses, and specified employer responsibilities with respect to monitoring employee electronic activities. It actually increased the burden on the government and restricted the reporting requirements with respect to electronic surveillance. (The Electronic Communications Privacy Act of 1986 was amended in a similar fashion in 2000.)

Impact: policies, standards, guidelines, privacy, and monitoring.

The Electronic Communications Privacy Act of 1986, 2000

This law made it illegal for a person to intentionally access, without proper authorization, a facility through which an electronic communication service is provided or to intentionally exceed an authorization to access that facility with the result of obtaining, altering, or preventing authorized access to a wire or electronic communication while it is in electronic storage or transmission. For more information, see http://www4.law.cornell.edu/uscode/18/2701.html.

Impact: policies, standards, guidelines, privacy, and monitoring.

The Gramm Leach Bliley (GLB) Act of 1999 (Financial Services Modernization Act)

This law prohibits financial institutions from disclosing nonpublic personal information about customers unless the customer was given an opportunity to opt out. It also prohibits financial institutions from obtaining financial information about customers under false pretenses, and it requires both initial and ongoing disclosure of the institution's privacy policy and changes to it. For more information, see http://www.senate.gov/~banking/conf/confrpt.htm and http://www.ftc.gov/privacy/glbact/.

Impact: policies, standards, guidelines, privacy, and architecture.

The Electronic Freedom of Information Act of 1996

The act adjusted existing FOI law to ensure that not only paper records, but electronic records also fall under the aegis of FOIA. The statutory definition was expanded to specifically include federal records and information maintained electronically, including databases, e-mail, personal computers, diskettes, and CD-ROMs. The amendment was intended to broaden the public's access to federal records by placing frequently requested information online, in theory making it easier for the public and businesses using computers to get the information they need. The revised law stipulated that agencies shall provide records in any form or format requested by the person, if the record is readily reproducible by that agency in that form or format. For more information, see http://www.epa.gov/pesticides/foia/efoia.htm and http://thomas.loc.gov/cgi-bin/query/z?c104:H.R.3802.ENR.

Impact: policy, procedures, standards, and privacy.

The Healthcare Insurance Portability and Accountability Act (HIPAA) of 1996

Two components of HIPAA are applicable to digital security: the HIPAA Privacy Rule and the HIPAA Security Rule. The Privacy Rule identifies standards to protect individuals' personal healthcare information. These standards address patient control over personal information, set boundaries for use of the records, establish appropriate controls that must be used to protect information, and attempt to hold violators accountable for actions. The Privacy Rule was published in April of 2001 and must be complied with by April of 2003. The Security Rule outlines requirements for security administration, physical safeguards, and technical security, services, and mechanisms. The Security Rule has not been finalized and published. For additional information, see http://www.hcfa.gov/medicaid/hipaa/content/ HIPAASTA.pdf or http://www.hcfa.gov/medicaid/hipaa/content/more.asp.

Impact: privacy, policies, procedures, standards, asset management, physical security, continuity planning, security planning, architecture, operations, and monitoring.

The National Information Infrastructure Protection Act of 1996

This law amended the Computer Fraud and Abuse Act of 1986. It includes clarifications and adjustments of wordings to bring the prior legislation up to date with respect to new technology and its usage, and reclassifies crime labels placed on offenders. To summarize some of the classifications:

- It is no longer a crime for authorized users to inflict reckless or negligent damage to a system, however it is a felony if they inflict intentional damage.
- It is now a felony for trespassers to inflict intentional or reckless damage to a system.
- It is a misdemeanor for a trespasser to inflict negligent damages to a system. For additional information, see: http://www.usdoj.gov/ criminal/cybercrime/1030_anal.html.

Impact: policies, standards, guidelines, and monitoring.

The Computer Security Act of 1987

This act declared Congress's direction to improve security and privacy of sensitive information in federal computer systems. It declared the National Bureau of Standards as the party responsible for developing standards and guidelines with the support of the National Security Agency. Furthermore, it declared the requirements of security planning, privacy policies for information in federal computer systems, and training for users of sensitive federal computer systems.For additional information, see http://www.epic.org/crypto/csa/csa.html.

Impact: policies, standards, guidelines, and privacy.

The Computer Fraud and Abuse Act of 1986

The Computer Fraud and Abuse Act of 1986 was signed into law in order to clarify definitions of criminal fraud and abuse for federal computer crimes and to remove the legal ambiguities and obstacles to prosecuting these crimes. The act established two new felony offenses for the unauthorized access of "federal interest" computers and a misdemeanor for unauthorized trafficking in computer passwords. For additional information, see http://www.panix.com/~eck/computer-fraud-act. html or http://www.digitalcentury.com/encyclo/update/comfraud.html.

Impact: policies, standards, guidelines, and monitoring.

The Computer Crime Control Act of 1984

The law prohibits the unauthorized use of computers to obtain classified or private financial information, to gain unauthorized access to federal computers, to commit fraud, to transmit computer viruses, or to conduct fraudulent trafficking in computer passwords. For additional information, see http://www.usdoj.gov/criminal/cybercrime/s982.pdf.

Impact: policies, standards, guidelines, and monitoring.

U.S. Federal Privacy Act of 1974

This act addresses the following issues with regard to federal agencies:

- Conditions of disclosure of personal records, accurate accounting of certain disclosures, an individual's access to their personal records, maintaining personal records that are pertinent to or necessary for agency business, notification to individuals if their records are requested by others, and the rights of legal guardians to information about their wards. For additional information and the entire act, see http://www.usdoj.gov/foia/privstat.htm.

Impact: policies, standards, guidelines, and privacy

U.S. REGULATIONS, AGENCIES, AND GUIDELINES

The National Infrastructure Assurance Council (NIAC, 1999)

This council was established in an effort to promote partnership between the federal government and the private industries that own the nation's critical infrastructures. The NIAC provides the president with reports on infrastructure protection and was intended to propose and develop ways to encourage private industry to perform periodic risk assessments of critical processes, monitor development of Private Sector Information Sharing and Analysis Centers (PSISACs), and provide recommendations to the National Coordinator and the National Economic Council. For additional information, see http://www.ncs.gov/n5_hp/Customer_Service/XAffairs/NewService/NCS9953.htm.

Impact: policies, standards, guidelines, physical security, and planning.

Federal Guidelines for Searching and Seizing Computers (U.S. Dept. of Justice, 2001)

This publication supersedes all existing federal guidelines, and provides updated information regarding federal searches and seizures of computers and electronic information that may be used in the commission or planning of criminal activity. For additional information, see http://www.usdoj.gov/criminal/cybercrime/searchmanual.htm.

Impact: policies, and monitoring.

INTERNATIONAL LAWS, REGULATIONS, AND GUIDELINES RELATED TO DIGITAL SECURITY AND PRIVACY

Australia

Crimes Act: Part VIA—Offences Relating to Computers and Copyrights Act. For additional information, see http://scaleplus.law.gov.au/.

European Union

Directive 94/ /EC on the Protection of Individuals with Regard to the Processing of Personal Data and on the Free Movement of Such Data. For additional information, see http://www.privacy.org/pi/intl_orgs/ec/final_EU_Data_Protection.html.

India

Information Technology Act, June 2000. For additional information, see http://www.mit.gov.in/it-bill.htm.

Japan

Unauthorized Computer Access Law, February 2000. For additional information, see http://www.npa.go.jp/hightech/fusei_ac2/UCAlaw.html. Computer Crime Act. For additional information, see http://www.isc.meiji.ac.jp/~sumwel_h/Codes/comp-crim.htm.

Malaysia

The Computer Crime Act, April 1997. For additional information, see http://www.ktkm.gov.my/organisation/jurisdiction.html.

Mauritius

Information Technology Act 1998; Section 4: Criminal Code Amended. §369A. Computer Misuse; Telecommunications Act 1998; and Copy-

right Act 1997. For additional information, see http://ncb.intnet.mu/
mitt.htm.

Philippines

Electronic Commerce Act. For additional information, see http://www.
abogadomo.com/.

Poland

Amended Criminal Code, 1997; and Personal Data Protection Act,
1997.

United Kingdom

Computer Misuse Act, 1990; Data Protection Acts, 1994 & 1998;
Telecommunications (Fraud) Act, 1997; and Copyright, Designs and
Patents Act, 1998. For additional information, see http://www.tsonline.
co.uk/portal.asp and http://www.mcconnellinternational.com/services/
Updatedlaws.htm.

Appendix B

Threat Vectors

A ny list of top threats is subject to change as technology advances and new threats and vulnerabilities emerge. As of November 2002, this is the list of the top 10 digital security threat vectors, as compiled by the security experts at Ernst & Young's Advanced Security Centers. There remains many other risks to digital security, some of which are listed in the Glossary.

2002 TOP 10 DIGITAL SECURITY THREAT VECTORS

1. *Digital infrastructure attacks:* Attacks against the systems that enable networks to communicate, such as routers, gateways, and switches, continue to increase. This allows individuals to scale attacks and impact many users by taking out the glue that holds networks together. It is a far more effective method of attack than attacking individual computers.
2. *Attack propagation:* In the past, attack methods required a person to initiate an attack against a specific target or set of targets. The one person to one attack target scenario has been superseded by attack tools that can self-initiate additional attack

cycles. Attacks such as Code Red and Nimda self-propagated to a point of global saturation in less than 18 hours.

3. *Patch timing:* The large volume of vulnerabilities and increased frequency of new vulnerabilities being discovered have made it extremely challenging for organizations to install patches within a feasible timeframe. The time between discovery of the vulnerability and the organization's implementation of a patch provides a window of opportunity for hackers to attack.

4. *Evading radar:* It is becoming increasingly difficult to distinguish between attack signatures and normal network traffic. This difficulty is due to the sophistication of the tools available to hackers and the ability of the signatures to blend in with a stream of authorized activity.

5. *Distributed tools:* Distributed attack tools are capable of launching denial-of-service attacks more efficiently, scanning for potential victims and compromising vulnerable systems. Coordination tools such as instant messaging (IM) allow for an instant exchange of information related to vulnerable networks.

6. *Dynamic payload:* In the past, attacks were performed in defined sequential steps. Today's attack methodologies can change their patterns and behavior based on random selection and target profile.

7. *Multipurpose tools:* Tools in the past were developed with one specific attack in mind. Today, tools can be quickly reengineered to take advantage of the latest discovered vulnerability. Usually these tools are developed to work on a variety of operating systems or platforms.

8. *Antifootprint techniques:* Digital activities normally leave footprints within system logs. Attackers are using techniques to erase log entries, making the identification of their presence on a network much more challenging.

9. *Wireless technology:* The increased use of wireless technology has introduced another risk vector to corporate IT networks.

Wireless technology typically is deployed without a thorough understanding of available security countermeasures.

10. *Mobile devices:* Today's computing environment takes on several forms, including personal digital assistants (PDAs), cell phones, pagers, laptops, key-chain-size storage devices, and traditional servers and workstations. As new technology is introduced, the digital security perimeter becomes extremely fluid and more difficult to protect.

APPENDIX C

Ernst & Young 2002 Digital Security Overview: An Executive Guide and Diagnostic

The Ernst & Young LLP Security & Technology Solutions practice recently commissioned MarketOne International to conduct a study of major North American corporations to determine the state of digital security issues in today's marketplace. The study was conceived to determine the state of digital security preparedness in some of the world's largest firms, and to determine how close those companies are to having in place digital security programs that can be described as "world-class." The results of the Digital Security Overview will serve as a baseline for future studies.

In April, 2002, ninety-one Fortune 500® firms representing twelve industry groupings agreed to provide detailed information regarding their existing and planned digital security programs. The respondent groups were consolidated into six major industry groupings: Technology and Media; Financial Services, which includes banking, insurance, and brokerage firms; Automotive and Industrial Manufacturing; Energy, which includes the oil and gas industries as well as utilities; Telecommunications; and Life Sciences, which includes pharmaceutical firms. Each of the consolidated industry groupings included a minimum of ten companies.

The study sampled was diverse in terms of size and scope, and consisted of a good cross-section of major North American business organizations. Approximately one-third of the firms had fewer than 10,000 employees, one-third had more than 50,000, and several had more than 250,000 employees. One-fifth of respondent companies had annual revenues of less than $1 billion; one-fifth had revenues in excess of $20 billion.

The individuals interviewed for this study hold executive or senior-level management positions in their respective firms, and all are direct decisionmakers with regard to digital security issues. The questions for this index were drafted, tested, implemented, and scored appropriately with regard to the definition of world-class digital security, which is described below. The scoring mechanism involved combining the scores on a matrix that looked at the nine Security Agenda Items across the six Characteristics of a world-class digital security program. The maximum score indicated a world-class digital security program was in place.

Many recent studies of digital security provide solid information regarding the rewards of having digital security programs in place, and the risks of not having them in place. For instance, the 2002 CSI/FBI Computer Crime and Security Survey, the CIO Magazine 2001 Security Worksheet, the Ernst & Young Global Information Security Survey 2002, and other research published by PriceWaterhouseCoopers, Gartner, and Deloitte & Touche provide statistics indicating the number digital security incidents has risen over time, and the frequency and severity of the incidents are increasing, as are the costs of responding to them.

The Ernst & Young Digital Security Overview goes a step further. The purpose of this study was not to reiterate information about the risks or the rewards related to digital security. The purpose was to gather in-depth information regarding major organizations' total security framework by assessing their preparedness to face a security incident. This study documents the root causes of vulnerabilities or security shortfalls—not just the symptoms, and not just the results.

By showing where industries stand with regard to digital security, this study enables CIOs and CSOs to determine *why* their organizations are vulnerable, *where* their organizations are vulnerable, and *what needs to be changed* to address those vulnerabilities. In short, this index provides a roadmap that enables digital security programs to achieve the distinction "world-class."

The expression "world-class" is used to describe an organization with a digital security program that addresses a Security Agenda composed of nine Items that address broad security issues. Each of the nine Items comprises specific security components and functions. The nine Items are Intrusion and Virus Detection; Incident Response; Privacy; Policies, Standards, and Guidelines; Physical Security; Asset and Service Management; Vulnerability Management; Entitlement Management; and Business Continuity.

Having these nine Items in place enables an organization to achieve an on-going cycle of asset protection. It means the organization has developed a technical architecture and internal mechanisms that enable control and containment capabilities that lead to risk reduction and management. It means that the organization has all the programs in place to achieve world-class digital security. However, within the definitions applied by this index, firms having all nine Items in place could not be identified as actually having "world-class" digital security programs unless the implementation of each Item could be described as aligned, enterprise-wide, continuous, proactive, validated, and formal. When the "weave" of fully deployed Agenda Items and fully realized Characteristics has been achieved, as shown in Figure C.1, an organization's digital security program can be described as "world class."

There are degrees of digital security. There are not degrees of world-class digital security. The epitome of a world-class digital security program is superiority in all areas, and by defining "world class" as such, the Ernst & Young Digital Security Overview set the bar high.

The results of this study are revealing, and the greatest revelation they provide is that world-class digital security is achievable although few companies have achieved that distinction. As will be presented below, many industries are well prepared to face certain incidents; others are less so. But the difference between being world-class and not being world-class is the difference between enduring two hours of website downtime during an incident or twelve, or between discovering an attempted entry by an unauthorized user and discovering the organization's confidential network was penetrated an hour ago by a well-known hacker named "KleptoPacketMonkey."

FIGURE C.1   World-Class Digital Security

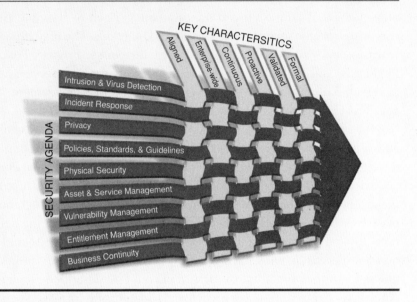

In the last few years, or even the last decade, the corporate security mindset has changed from a "what if . . . ?" perspective to an "if . . . then" perspective. The inevitability of an incident occurring has become accepted, and the ability of an organization to react adequately has allowed a false, smug confidence to pervade the marketplace. Such confidence is naïve and has no place in the real world. Organizations must be prepared to respond—not react—to a digital security incident, because the more prepared an organization is, the more successfully it will be able to absorb the impact. That is what the Security Agenda Items are all about: absorbing the impact because the impact cannot be avoided.

The results are presented by Agenda Item, and industry averages are presented for each Item. Briefly, the scoring mechanism used in this index relied on highly detailed questions that addressed specific issues and practices related to Security Agenda Items in a corporate setting. Sixty-six questions were asked, and time was allowed for detailed explanations and follow-up questions on the respondents' part. A subset of twenty-nine of those questions were weighted according to their importance with regard to Security Agenda. The highest possible aggregate score is 75; the highest score possible on the Agenda Items is 45 and the highest possible for Characteristics is 30. The highest score a single company achieved with regard to Agenda Items was 44; the lowest was 9.375. The highest score a single company achieved for Characteristics was 29.25 and the lowest was 3.88.

While the results will be discussed in greater detail, the following set of tables presents an overview of the findings. Table C.1 presents the overall picture by industry. Tables C.2 and C.3 present overall average Agenda Item scores and industry average scores for Agenda Items, respectively. Tables C.4 and C.5 present overall average scores and industry average scores for Characteristics, respectively.

TABLE C.1   Combined Characteristics and Agenda Items: Industry Averages

Total Scores	Index Average	Auto/ Man	Energy	Financial Services	Life Sciences	Tech/ Media	Telecom
Agenda Items	30.77	30.11	28.09	31.61	29.36	30.69	34.23
Characteristics	20.63	20.55	18.43	21.55	19.64	20.35	23.33
Aggregate	51.40	50.66	46.52	53.16	49.00	51.04	57.56

TABLE C.2   Agenda Item Average Scores

Agenda Item	Average Score (Mean)	High Score	Low Score
Intrusion Detection System	3.53	5.00	0.00
Incident Response	3.79	5.00	0.50
Privacy	3.62	5.00	0.00
Policies, Standards, Guidelines	3.16	4.75	0.00
Physical Security	3.24	5.00	0.00
Asset Management	3.75	5.00	1.50
Entitlement Management	2.90	4.75	0.00
Vulnerability Management	3.13	5.00	0.00
Business Continuity	3.66	4.75	0.00

The overall mean was 30.77. The overall median score was 31.50. The highest score for an individual company was 44.00 and the lowest was 9.38.

TABLE C.3   Agenda Item Average Scores by Industry

Agenda Item	Index Average	Auto/ Man	Energy	Financial Services	Life Sciences	Tech/ Media	Telecom
Intrusion Detection System	3.53	2.84	3.48	3.83	2.83	3.76	3.90
Incident Response	3.79	3.66	3.39	4.11	3.90	3.84	3.93
Privacy	3.62	3.59	2.77	4.11	3.13	3.44	4.25
Policies, Standards, Guidelines	3.16	3.36	2.95	3.29	2.81	3.32	3.49
Physical Security	3.24	3.18	2.43	3.10	3.45	3.52	3.51
Asset Management	3.75	3.50	3.82	3.72	3.65	3.79	4.05
Entitlement Management	2.90	2.91	2.89	2.58	2.58	2.93	3.60
Vulnerability Management	3.13	3.18	2.50	2.16	3.58	2.82	3.58
Business Continuity	3.66	3.89	3.86	3.72	3.45	3.26	3.93
Total Score	30.77	30.11	28.09	31.61	29.36	30.69	34.23

TABLE C.4   Characteristic Average Score

Characteristic	Average Score (Mean)	High Score	Low Score
Aligned	3.45	5.00	0.75
Enterprise-Wide	3.33	5.00	0.00
Continuous	3.53	5.00	0.50
Proactive	3.08	5.00	0.50
Validated	3.59	5.00	0.63
Formal	3.65	5.00	0.50

The overall mean was 20.63. The overall median score was 21.00. The highest score for an individual company was 29.25 and the lowest was 3.88.

TABLE C.5   Characteristic Average Scores by Industry

Characteristic	Index Sample	Auto/ Man	Energy	Financial Services	Life Sciences	Tech/ Media	Telecom
Aligned	3.45	3.59	2.77	3.72	2.95	3.41	4.15
Enterprise-Wide	3.33	3.18	2.77	3.35	3.00	3.51	3.94
Continuous	3.53	3.41	3.16	3.52	4.05	3.31	4.13
Proactive	3.08	2.91	3.00	3.03	2.88	3.03	3.40
Validated	3.59	3.82	3.48	3.84	3.29	3.49	3.84
Formal	3.65	3.64	3.25	4.09	3.48	3.60	3.88
Total Score	20.63	20.55	18.43	21.55	19.64	20.35	23.33

THE AGENDA ITEMS

With regard to the nine Agenda Items addressed in this index, respondents exhibited the highest level of preparedness in terms of having in place Incident Response programs, and exhibited the lowest level of preparedness in terms of having effective Entitlement Management programs in place. This can be interpreted as indicating that organizations are more effective at responding to an incident than preventing one from taking place by implementing effective "gatekeeping" mechanisms. When broken out by industry group, more significant variations were observed.

The Telecom group exhibited high levels of preparedness for every solution, achieving the highest industry scores for seven of the nine Items. The Technology/Media and Financial Services groups presented above-average levels of preparedness for the majority of the Items, and the Life Sciences and Automotive/Manufacturing groups displayed low levels of preparedness for the majority of the Items. The Energy group presented the lowest overall scores, achieving below-average scores for seven of the nine Items and the lowest overall scores for three Items. These results indicate that some industries are more prepared in some areas than in others; however, the industries themselves drive these results in some instances.

Given the nature of the subject, it is not surprising that the Telecom industry group is well prepared in most areas whereas Energy is less so. Nearly every aspect of the Telecommunications industry relies heavily on digital collection, storage, and transfer of data, whereas the Energy industry is heavily physical infrastructure-intensive. The Energy group presented above-average scores with regard to Asset Management and Continuity and Availability, and its scores for Entitlement Management and Intrusion Detection were very close to the average across industries. The Financial Services group achieved the highest score overall for Incident Response, and its scores for Privacy and Intrusion Detection were significantly above average. Again, this may have to do with the nature of this regulated industry.

Intrusion and Virus Detection

Sample question from the study: Does your company have an Intrusion Detection System?

	Auto/Man.	Energy	Financial Services	Life Sciences	Tech/Media	Telecom	All
Yes	64%	82%	94%	80%	82%	100%	86%
No	36%	18%	6%	20%	18%	0%	14%

Knowing the identity of system users and the permissions they've been granted is a fundamental issue in systems administration. If there is no way of knowing who is allowed access to the system and what they're allowed to do, there is no way of knowing who doesn't belong there or who is engaging in suspicious behavior. The ability to detect and isolate an intruder or an authorized user who has circumvented applied controls is a basic requirement of any digital security program. It is not surprising, therefore, that most firms consider the ability to detect and isolate an intrusion to be a high priority. This is borne out by the survey: a significant majority of respondents reported that they have an Intrusion Detection System.

However, the results also show some unsettling discrepancies: companies that have an Intrusion Detection System in place as a proactive measure are not deploying it enterprise-wide, which therefore limits the system's utility and effectiveness. Eleven percent of the companies with an Intrusion Detection System in place actively monitor less than 25% of their critical servers for intrusions, and 16% of the companies actively monitor less than 25% of their Internet and Extranet connections for intrusions. Only 42% of respondents indicated they monitor 95 to 100% of their critical servers, and only 35% percent indicated that they monitor 95 to 100% of their Internet and Extranet connections for intrusions.

The industry-specific figures are more surprising than the aggregate numbers. Thirty-eight percent of the Life Sciences group indicated that they actively monitor less than 25% of their critical servers, and 27% percent of the Financial Services industry group actively monitor less than 25% of their Internet and Extranet monitors. Only 20% of Telecom respondents indicated they monitored critical servers and Internet and Extranet connections at the 95 to 100% level. Eighteen percent of Energy industry respondents indicated that they monitored 95 to 100% of their critical servers, and only 9% indicated they monitored 95 to 100% of their Intranet and Extranet connections.

Across industry groups, three-quarters of the companies without an Intrusion Detection System in place gave one of two reasons for the omission: they "have not been shown the value or ROI of implementing an Intrusion Detection System," or they had not allocated sufficient resources "to implement, monitor, and maintain an Intrusion Detection System."

Resource allocation appears to be an issue even among companies with an Intrusion Detection System in place. Three-quarters of the companies with an Intrusion Detection System in place have fewer than 10 employees dedicated full-time to managing the system. This is surprising, given that more than two-thirds of respondent companies have more than 10,000 employees. Only 3% of respondents have more than 100 employees dedicated full-time to managing their Intrusion Detection System.

To be considered world-class, a digital security program must include a fully deployed Intrusion and Detection System. By having a system and not deploying it, a company is begging for trouble. It is doubtful that, should an incident occur, shareholders and consumers would be understanding about having put their trust or their money in the hands of an organization that refused to protect its own resources. There is, perhaps, one instance in which monitoring 25% of critical servers is acceptable, and that is if one of those servers being monitored is the one someone tries to hack. However, leaving critical servers unprotected, or at least unwatched, is not cost-effective if an incident occurs, and as has been discussed, an incident *will* occur.

Incident Response

Sample question from the study: Which of the following best characterizes the level of detail that is provided in your organization's Incident Response Plan?

	Auto/Man	Energy	Financial Services	Life Sciences	Tech/Media	Telecom	All
A complete detailed document with roles and procedures	37%	37%	81%	40%	47%	40%	47%
A high-level document	27%	27%	13%	40%	35%	50%	31%
A call list	27%	18%	0%	10%	12%	0%	14%
None	9%	18%	6%	10%	6%	10%	8%

A security incident can be many things. Not all of them are malicious, but all are potentially damaging. The actions of hackers and the impact of viruses have been widely reported in the media. However, the more common and continual problems do not get reported. These include policy violations, unauthorized use of networks or systems, attempts to gain unauthorized access to data or systems, and unauthorized attempts to change or delete information within a system. They also include employees who write down new passwords, then leave them taped to the front of their monitors; a former employee who retains access to systems; a new employee who erroneously posts confidential data on a public website. All of these scenarios, and many more, can be classified as security incidents.

Although a vast majority of Automotive/ Manufacturing respondents perceived an unauthorized intrusion or major virus to be a high threat, only half of the aggregate did. Likewise, approximately half the overall respondents perceived employee misconduct involving organizational networks to be a mid-level threat, although such misconduct is much more common than an external threat.

More than half the respondents described the risk associated with a digital security incident as being "a major risk that would seriously affect the organization," and more than a third described the risk as something that "would not seriously affect the organization." Only one-quarter of the Financial Services firms described the risk of a computer incident as "a grave risk that would cripple and possibly destroy the organization." These results show a tendency to overlook commonplace threats in favor of high-profile events, and to downplay the risk of an incident overall.

The actions the respondent companies are taking to mitigate risks and respond to them when they occur are in line with their stated concerns, but their efforts are not as effective as they could be. One-third of companies have established acceptable-use policies addressing company networks and have explained them to employees; however, only 11% acknowledge having developed Incident Response policies and procedures for internal threats.

Fewer than half of respondents described their overall Incident Response Plans as being "a complete document that defines an incident, documents threat alert categories and escalation procedures, details roles and responsibilities, and contains incident scenarios, investigative steps, and system resumption strategies."

Slightly more than one-third of respondents in the Automotive/ Manufacturing and Energy groups described their plans as such; however, 81% of Financial Services companies indicated that a complete document was in use. Overall, 14% of respondents described their Incident Response Plan as a phone call "tree." Ten percent of organizations admitted they didn't have an Incident Response Plan, and 18% of Energy respondents admitted the same.

When a digital security incident does occur, approximately one-third of respondent organizations inform corporate officers, who are responsible for any resulting business decisions; another third inform division-level managers, who are then responsible for any resulting business decisions. Ten percent of respondents indicated that no formal process requiring executive-level involvement exists.

A world-class digital security program must have in place an Incident Response program that is proactive in its approach, widely disseminated and understood, and validated by formal, thorough, and continuous testing. A program that is aligned with business objectives and that has lent a high priority to enterprise-wide awareness of Incident Response protocols will have guidelines in place that direct appropriate behavior during and after an incident occurs.

Privacy

Sample question from the study: On a scale of 1 to 5, with 1 being very confident and 5 being unconfident, where would you place your firm with regard to the following privacy practices?

	Auto/Man	Energy	Financial Services	Life Sciences	Tech/Media	Telecom
Only collect customer information according to privacy policy	1.7	1.3[g]	1.8	1.9[f]	1.5[d]	1.3
Only use or share customer information in accordance with privacy policies	1.7	1.9[e]	1.7	2[c]	1.7[d]	1.4
Have internal controls and procedures to ensure only authorized persons can access customer data	2.3	2.1[a]	1.9	2	1.8	1.5
Security procedures are in place to protect personal data from outside hackers or intruders	1.8	1.7[a]	1.7	1.8	1.6	1.2
Do not release customers' personal data to 3rd parties without the express consent of the consumer or if required by law	1.3	1.1[e]	1.7	1.5[c]	1.5	1.3
Ensure the use of customer information by 3rd parties complies with the privacy policies	2.1	1.4[g]	1.9	2.3[f]	1.4[b]	1.6

a—9% did not know   d—24% did not know   g—36% did not know
b—18% did not know   e—27% did not know
c—20% did not know   f—30% did not know

Conducting business in a digitally interconnected economy requires incorporating privacy safeguards into operations at all levels, particularly information systems. The degree to which an organization chooses to adhere to increasingly stringent privacy standards will determine whether its privacy policies are a competitive advantage or a potential risk. Organizations must balance the need to maximize the utility of the private information they possess while building and maintaining trust and confidence among stakeholders. The Privacy Agenda Item includes enterprise-wide controls and proactive countermeasures supported by formal policies to ensure that only authorized users gain access to private data.

Results of this study indicate that regulatory issues drive much of the attention given to Privacy. More than half of respondents indicated that the primary reason for addressing the issue of Information Privacy was regulatory compliance. One-quarter indicated that risk management was the primary reason.

Not surprisingly, the issue of regulatory compliance was particularly pronounced in the Financial Services and Life Sciences industries, which are held under more scrutiny with regard to Privacy than are other industry groups surveyed. While, overall, only 12% of respondents cited customer expectations as the primary driver for addressing Privacy concerns, within the Telecom industry group 30% indicated such. Twenty-six percent of respondents overall indicated that they have had independent auditors validate adherence to their Privacy policies. However, the same percentage of respondents deemed such a step "unnecessary." Twenty-nine percent are assessing the need for third-party validation of Privacy policies, and 18% are in the process of implementing it.

Fewer than half of respondents indicated that a formal Chief Privacy Officer position does not exist within their organizations, and variations by industry were significant. Seventy percent of Telecom respondents indicated they did not have a formal Privacy Officer position, and 65% of Technology/Media companies indicated such. By contrast, only one-third of Life Sciences companies did not have such an office. In companies in which such a position does exist, the majority of them are aligned with the Corporate Legal Department. This is particularly pronounced within the Financial Services and Energy industries; however, nearly a third of Energy respondents indicated that the Privacy Officer reported into the Risk Management group.

Privacy is an area of growing concern for all industries as regulatory bodies struggle to balance the need for fluidity in the marketplace and the need to protect individuals' private information. An enterprise-wide Privacy program that is aligned to business goals and is validated to ensure compliance with regulatory standards will enable organizations to achieve that balance more successfully.

Policies, Standards, and Guidelines

Sample question from the study: To what degree are your information security policies designed to cover the domains defined by ISO 17799, CISSP, Common Criteria, or another recognized model?

	Auto/Man	Energy	Financial Services	Life Sciences	Tech/Media	Telecom	All
All necessary policies must comply	46%	27%	44%	0%	41%	40%	34%
Most necessary policies must comply	36%	46%	31%	50%	41%	10%	36%
Some necessary policies must comply	9%	9%	25%	50%	12%	0%	20%
Most policies do not comply	0%	9%	0%	0%	0%	30%	5%
No compliance	9%	9%	0%	0%	6%	20%	5%

Sample question from the study: How would you characterize your information security policies with regard to being supported by documented procedures and guidelines for all users?

	Auto/Man	Energy	Financial Services	Life Sciences	Tech/Media	Telecom	All
They are documented, implemented, and followed	9%	9%	31%	30%	29%	30%	21%
They are documented; some implemented and followed	64%	46%	50%	10%	41%	50%	45%
They are documented; not implemented or followed	0%	18%	0%	20%	0%	20%	9%
Some documented, implemented, and followed	27%	27%	13%	40%	24%	0%	22%
They are not documented	0%	0%	6%	0%	6%	0%	3%

Having in place comprehensive Policies, Standards, and Guidelines that have been validated and are reviewed and updated regularly enables an organization to proactively plan, manage, and respond to information security risks, threats, and vulnerabilities. No digital security program can be described as being world-class without a policy development and implementation structure in place. Such a structure is the communication link between executive management and the digital security team, and the personnel who rely on that team to carry out functions.

The development and implementation of Policies, Standards, and Guidelines is a cause of concern for most respondents, with 25% of them naming it as their greatest challenge. Within the Energy and Automotive/Manufacturing industry groups, 36% of respondents designated it as their greatest challenge. However, overall, the results indicate that, whether with regard to content or deployment issues, organizational Policies, Standards, and Guidelines are not being viewed by companies from the perspective of being proactive, formal, and continuous components of a digital security program.

When respondents were asked about specific issues that would be addressed or included in their digital security plan, not a single issue garnered a 100% inclusion rate. In other words, there was not one issue that all organizations considered significant enough to include. Incident Response planning garnered the highest inclusion rate, which was 88%. Eighty-seven percent of respondents indicated their plans would include or address formal reviews of security controls, roles and responsibilities, personnel security, and security awareness training. Less than 80% of the respondents indicated that Business Continuity plans, hardware, applications, systems software maintenance controls, and physical and environmental protections would be addressed or included in their digital security plans.

Overall results indicate that companies do not place a high priority on having a digital security policy structure that is aligned with current business processes and risk strategy and is maintained in a continuous fashion. Only 10% of respondents review their digital security policies for consistency with organizational objectives on a monthly basis. Sixty-five percent review them at least once per year, and 4% rarely or never review them. Twenty percent review their security policies when a perceived need arises.

Considerable variation exists between and among industries, however. Within the Automotive/Manufacturing industry group, 36% review security policies monthly; however, the same percentage of that industry group review them only when a perceived need arises. Within the Energy group, 45% review annually, 27% review when a perceived need arises, and 18% rarely or never review them. Within the Financial Services industry, more than half review annually and a third when a perceived need arises. The "high-tech" industries had slightly better success with review cycles. Within the Technology/Media industry, 41% review at least twice per year and 35% review once per year; among Telecom respondents, 40% review at least twice per year and half review once per year.

Ensuring their policies are validated to established guidelines also appears to be a low priority for many organizations. When asked if their digital security policies cover the domains defined by recognized models such as ISO 17799, CISSP, Common Criteria, or others, only one-third of respondents indicated complete compliance. However, almost one-half of the Automotive/Manufacturing group indicated complete compliance. Fifteen percent of respondents overall indicated little or no compliance.

The issues of how well and how thoroughly digital security policies are being documented, deployed, implemented, administered, and followed appear to be problematic across most industries. Only 21% of the responding companies have formal digital security policies that are supported by documented procedures and guidelines for all users. Nearly half stated that all policies are documented but not fully implemented or followed. Nine percent indicated that policies are documented but not implemented or followed.

Again, considerable variation exists between and among industries. Seventy-three percent of Automotive/ Manufacturing respondents acknowledged having fully documented policies, however only 9% stated that their policies were also implemented and followed. All Energy industry respondents indicated that at least some of their policies were documented, but only 9% indicated their policies were documented, implemented, and followed. Eighty-one percent of Financial Services firms reported full documentation with varying degrees of implementation and adherence, and nearly one-third have policies that are documented, implemented, and followed. Sixty percent of Life Sciences, 75% of Telecom respondents, and 70% of Tech/Media respondents indicated full documentation with varying degrees of implementation and adherence.

Attempting universal deployment, monitoring, and administration of digital security policies appears to be a significant challenge for the majority of respondents. Only 18% were able to describe their attempts to do so as "successful and complete." Seventy-one percent acknowledged attempting universal deployment with varying degrees of administration and monitoring. Twelve percent indicated they had made no attempt at universal deployment of digital security policies.

Considerable variation appeared among industry groups with regard to the issue of deployment and supporting activities. All respondents in the Telecom, Energy, and Life Sciences industry groups attempted universal deployment. The Telecom industry had the highest degree of success with 40% achieving complete success with regard to universal deployment, monitoring, and administration. More than one-third of Energy respondents made some effort with regard to administration and monitoring, while 45% made no effort. More than one-quarter of respondents in the Automotive/ Manufacturing group made no attempt at universal deployment. Nearly half of all respondents indicated that policy compliance is monitored and administered in an ad hoc fashion.

The widely disparate results among and between industry groups indicate that developing policies and ensuring they are effectively deployed and maintained are significant challenges for many companies in many industries. Overall, it appears that the regulated industries have better success at deployment. However, they do not display exceptional rigor with regard to ensuring those policies are effectively monitored and administered. Without a comprehensive Policies, Standards, and Guidelines Agenda Item in place to ensure that organizational security objectives are aligned to business objectives, deployed enterprise-wide, and continuously maintained and validated, the digital security program will be incomplete.

Physical Security

Sample question from the study: Which of the following areas are addressed by your organization's physical security policy?

	Auto/ Man	Energy	Financial Services	Life Sciences	Tech/Media	Telecom	All
Laptop/PC computer security	100%	64%	81%	80%	88%	100%	85%
Handling and securing sensitive document printing	64%	45%	75%	60%	82%	90%	71%
Handling and securing sensitive mail/mailboxes/mail slots	55%	64%	63%	50%	71%	80%	65%
Disposal of sensitive documents	73%	64%	88%	90%	82%	100%	80%

Physical measures, such as locks, bars, alarms, and uniformed guards, are fundamental to an organization's total security effort because they are key components of controlling access to digital assets. In a world-class digital security program, physical security efforts are in alignment with proactive, enterprise-wide digital security operations. An organization that ignores the physical aspect of digital security is leaving unaddressed a significant vulnerability.

Nearly three-quarters of respondents considered employee screening to be a high priority for their organizations. Approximately one-third consider physical access controls, such as restricted entry, and security awareness training to be a high priority. Physical access controls were considered a high priority by 88% of Financial Services firms. However, only 45% of Energy firms considered physical access controls to be a high priority, and 27% of Energy firms considered security guards and boundary protection to be a low priority. Only 12% of respondents over-all consider biometric controls to be a high priority.

When asked about specific proactive Physical Security practices, there was considerable variation among industry groups. Every respon-dent in the Telecom and Automotive/Manufacturing groups indicated that they had measures in place addressing Laptop/PC computer secu-rity; however, only 64% of Energy respondents did, and only 80% of Life Sciences respondents did. Eighty percent of respondents overall have addressed the disposal of sensitive documents, and 71% of respon-dents indicated that they have instituted measures addressing the han-dling and securing of sensitive documents printed on-site. Only 45% of Energy respondents have addressed secure printing issues. Proper han-dling and securing of sensitive mail, mailboxes, and mail slots have been addressed by only 65% of respondents.

Thirty percent of respondents conduct annual security awareness training, and 10% of respondents provide no security training at all. Within the Energy, Automotive/Manufacturing, and Financial Services industries, 18% of companies indicated that employees receive no phys-ical security training.

Physical security has become a fundamental component of overall corporate security. Organizations continue to seek digital methods to enhance productivity, and one result has been the introduction of addi-tional challenges to managing physical security. It is only when physical and digital security objectives are aligned that organizations can begin to effectively manage risks to digital assets. Protecting employees and company assets from unpredictable events is of increasing priority for senior management, which means a fully deployed, enterprise-wide Physical Security Agenda Item must be a critical component of any dig-ital security program.

Asset and Service Management

Sample question from the study: Which one of the following statements best describes the way your organization currently tracks physical assets?

	Auto/Man	Energy	Financial Services	Life Sciences	Tech/Media	Telecom	All
Manually, using a spreadsheet or document to track changes, moves, disposal of assets, and physical inventory	18%	18%	6%	0%	19%	0%	12%
Automatically, using asset management software to track assets and associated costs	46%	64%	38%	60%	55%	90%	54%
Partially automated, partially manual	36%	18%	56%	40%	26%	10%	34%
We do not track physical assets	0%	0%	0%	0%	0%	0%	0%

The goal of the Asset and Service Management Agenda Item is increased productivity. Mechanisms, procedures, and technologies that might improve productivity are measured in terms of potential utility and return on investment. It's difficult to dispute that knowing what assets are owned and where they are is highly useful knowledge to any organization, and that properly managing the assets' deployment and use carries with it a return on investment. Having in place streamlined mechanisms, such as fully automated asset tracking systems and automatically deployed application and system upgrades, can secure that return.

Respondents to our study understand the benefits of a strong Asset and Service Management program. Nearly three-quarters of them ranked "achieving a positive return on invested capital" as the highest benefit. Lowering the total cost of ownership on infrastructure assets, supporting disaster recovery and business continuity plans, and improving quality of service to internal customers were ranked "high" by more than half.

However, our study indicates that not all companies engage in behaviors that will allow them to reap those benefits. Less than one-fifth of the companies we interviewed define their corporate Asset Management strategy as entailing "a comprehensive repository containing asset portfolio, contract, and financial information as well as best practices business processes." The remaining firms place partial responsibility for maintaining asset information with the individual business units, the Information Technology department, and the Finance/Accounting department, indicating that other, additional internal groups or departments house different or additional information.

A slim majority of companies overall have deployed Asset Management software that tracks the assets and associated costs; however, 90%

of Telecom companies we surveyed have deployed such a tool. More than a tenth of respondents across the sample rely solely on manual methods, such as a spreadsheet, to track physical and digital assets. The remaining one-third of the sample, including more than half of the Financial Services companies, use hybrid methods. Respondents who don't use fully automated methods cited the following reasons with equal frequency: lack of internal resources, lack of a budget, and having no evidence of a compelling business reason to institute such a solution. Within the Financial Services industry, a majority cited a lack of internal resources. Within the Life Sciences industry, a majority cited budget constraints, and within the Technology/Media segment, a majority cited the lack of a compelling business case.

These reasons indicate the lack a proactive, enterprise-wide approach to Asset and Service Management, a lack of understanding that Asset and Service Management is more than maintaining equipment inventories and software licensing documentation. True, comprehensive Asset and Service Management entails the consolidation and centralization of information regarding all of an organization's assets: infrastructure, physical components, digital data, and intangibles. To be effective at an enterprise level, an Asset and Service Management program must be sponsored at the executive level and be fed information from many groups within the company, including Information Technology, Procurement, Financial, Human Resources, and others. A properly designed and implemented Asset and Service Management solution aligns an organization's personnel, mechanisms, and technologies with a management process to streamline the function of tracking assets and the cost of those assets.

When executives have at-a-glance access to asset information, they can better understand the total cost of ownership. A formal Asset and Service Management solution will show real benefits that can be measured in real terms. Enterprise-wide efficiencies can be achieved, which include increased productivity for Information Technology personnel and those relying on them, reduced downtime for assets, and improved customer service. Perhaps most importantly, the organization will be more secure if its assets are, and that is the true return on investment.

Vulnerability Management

Sample question from the study: In your opinion, which one of the following statements would best describe how effectively your organization manages system vulnerabilities?

	Auto/Man	Energy	Financial Services	Life Sciences	Tech/Media	Telecom	All
We have the ability to identify and track vulnerabilities as well as measure compliance	27%	9%	13%	30%	24%	20%	21%
We have wide-scale deployment of vulnerability tracking and knowledge of all critical infrastructure vulnerabilities	9%	9%	37%	10%	12%	20%	16%
Vulnerability information is obtained from various sources and administered on periodic basis	46%	64%	31%	40%	34%	60%	44%
Vulnerability management is adhoc and handled by IT or security staff alone	18%	0%	19%	20%	18%	0 %	15%
Vulnerability management has not been addressed	0%	18%	0%	0%	12%	0%	4%

Digital vulnerabilities and subsequent exploitations are constants in a digitally connected marketplace. They are difficult to discover and difficult to track, and therefore pose a huge, often hidden threat to the integrity of information systems. The only way to effectively address vulnerabilities is with a proactive, enterprise-wide methodology. The Vulnerability Management Agenda Item provides organizations with an integrated approach for centralized monitoring and automated methods of ensuring that compliance and secure configurations are maintained throughout the organization. This will result in an improved security profile and significant cost savings with regard to Incident Response.

The first step in an effective defense against unknown vulnerabilities is a detailed understanding of the organization's existing system and environmental vulnerabilities, and the variables that can change them. Because vulnerabilities can and do change quickly, Vulnerability Management is an issue of great concern for respondents. Nineteen percent of them named it as their second greatest challenge, behind having in place effective Policies, Standard, and Guidelines. The way in which many organizations assess their systems for known vulnerabilities appears to be a vulnerability in itself. Only 44% perform daily assessments, and 5% assess their systems only once per year. Only 21% of respondents stated they have the ability to identify and track vulnerabilities as well as measure compliance. Sixteen percent of respondents acknowledged that their organizations have in place "wide-scale deployment of vulnerability tracking and knowledge of all critical infrastructure vulnerabilities."

Within the Energy industry, 64% state that vulnerability information is obtained from various sources and administered on a periodic basis. Within the Financial Services industry, only 13% claim to have the ability to identify and track vulnerabilities as well as measure compliance. Thirty-seven percent state that they have wide-scale deployment of vulnerability tracking and knowledge of all critical infrastructure vulnerabilities, and 31% claim that vulnerability information is obtained from various sources and administered on periodic basis. Within the Technology/Media industry segment, 12% state that Vulnerability Management has not yet been addressed, and 18% of Energy respondents admit the same. Within the Telecom industry, 60% state that vulnerability information is obtained from various sources and administered on a periodic basis.

The ways in which many organizations disseminate information about vulnerabilities and address known system vulnerabilities appear less formal than they could be. Only slightly more than one-third of respondents acknowledge that operating groups disseminate vulnerability information, and slightly less than one-third of respondents indicate that it is the responsibility of every system administrator to research and patch his or her own system. Just over one-quarter of respondents indicate that the security administrator e-mails daily vulnerabilities to all Information Technology personnel, and individuals are responsible for patching their own systems.

Having in place the right Vulnerability Management Agenda Item means an organization has adopted broad, proactive methodologies that enable it to detect, deflect, and defuse security vulnerabilities. This translates into fewer security incidents occurring, and experiencing fewer incidents translates into less downtime, which means strong tangible and intangible returns on investment in a marketplace under near-continual digital threat.

Entitlement Management

Sample question from the study: Does your organization deploy secure e-mail, is it planning to deploy it, or is it neither deploying nor planning to deploy secure e-mail?

	Auto/Man	Energy	Financial Services	Life Sciences	Tech/Media	Telecom	All
Secure e-mail deployed	73%	55%	56%	60%	76%	60%	65%
Secure e-mail planned	9%	18%	38%	30%	12%	30%	22%
Neither	18%	27%	6%	10%	12%	10%	13%

Sample question from the study: Does your organization deploy centralized user authorization, authentication, or Policy Management tools, is it planning to deploy them, or is it neither deploying nor planning to deploy them?

	Auto/Man	Energy	Financial Services	Life Sciences	Tech/Media	Telecom	All
Tools deployed	45%	55%	25%	20%	65%	70%	47%
Deployment planned	45%	27%	69%	80%	23%	30%	45%
Neither	10%	18%	6%	0%	12%	0%	8%

Sample question from the study: Does your organization deploy Single Sign-On (SSO) technology, is it planning to deploy it, or is it neither deploying nor planning to deploy it?

	Auto/Man	Energy	Financial Services	Life Sciences	Tech/Media	Telecom	All
Tools deployed	36%	18%	13%	10%	44%	60%	30%
Deployment planned	36%	46%	62%	40%	25%	10%	40%
Neither	28%	36%	25%	50%	31%	30%	30%

The success and security of a digital enterprise rests on one issue: trust. It's a basic requirement in any digital transaction. Customers entrust an organization with private information, believing that the organization has in place effective, enterprise-wide safeguards that have been validated and are on-going. Managers must trust their employees to handle private information appropriately and apply the available safeguards. Executive management trusts that digital security decisions will be aligned with business objectives, and will support and enable enhanced productivity and performance.

Establishing trust in a digital environment requires the use of controls that allow, restrict, and monitor access to information and systems. Such controls can include user authorization and authentication systems, intrusion detection systems, smartcards, digital certificates, and biometrics, as well as many other devices and applications. According to nearly half of the respondents, the most influential factor when considering the adoption of new security solutions is risk management. Slightly more than one-fifth identified legal or regulatory pressures as the most influential factor, and the same percentage considered a business enabler the most influential factor. Only ten percent considered audit findings to be the key factor.

Determining which control is the best solution in a given situation depends as much on the reason the control is needed as the service being rendered. Many internal and external mission-critical organizational activities are taking place online in today's marketplace. Ninety-eight percent of companies surveyed provide company information online and nearly as many provide employee self-service features. More than two-thirds engage in document exchanges with business partners and in direct selling or marketing to customers.

Nearly half of respondent companies engage in financial transactions through an industry exchange. Most of the transactions mentioned here take place over the Internet, which is openly accessible to the public and is notoriously porous. Yet only 84% of companies surveyed have Intrusion Detection Systems deployed, and only 69% have Web access control or authorization protocols. Only 65% have secure e-mail deployed and another 22% have it planned, leaving 13% that admit it is neither in place nor planned. Fewer than one-third of respondents overall have deployed Single Sign-On technology, although the same percentage have it neither deployed nor planned. However, 60% of the Telecom respondents have deployed it.

Fewer than half of the companies surveyed have deployed centralized user authentication, authorization, or policy management procedures, although nearly as many have deployment planned.

User authentication, authorization, administration, and auditing—knowing who has gained access to a system, what they are allowed to do, and what they are actually doing—are more than critical elements of digital security. They are the very foundation of it. The Entitlement Management Agenda Item provides a secure gateway to an organization's systems. A properly designed, appropriately deployed, and efficiently maintained digital security program that has Entitlement Management as its base will reduce downtime and increase return on investment by deflecting security incidents from occurring in the first place, and providing critical data when they do occur.

Business Continuity

Sample question from the study: Typically, what is the PRIMARY means of ensuring that your business continuity/disaster recovery plans are current?

	Auto/Man	Energy	Financial Services	Life Sciences	Tech/Media	Telecom	All
Annual audit	82%	64%	75%	50%	53%	33%	59%
Occasional spot checks	0%	27%	25%	20%	29%	55%	24%
Updates are made following incidents	9%	0%	0%	0%	6%	0%	7%
Updating is outsourced to 3rd parties	0%	9%	0%	0%	12%	12%	2%
No method in place	9%	0%	0%	30%	0%	0%	8%

No one likes to think about disasters, but, natural or deliberate, physical or logical, they happen. In today's digitally interconnected world, threats can appear from virtually nowhere and an unprepared organization can be seriously compromised before the incident has been detected. The losses in terms of downtime and damage to brand and corporate image can be staggering. That is why it is vital that every organization have the ability to quickly and cost-effectively recover and restore critical systems, processes, and data. Organizations must have the ability to rapidly deploy personnel, processes, and technology to support the recovery of business operations and information systems.

The concept of Business Continuity and Disaster Recovery is not a new one, but it might as well be, given that only 13% of companies we surveyed have formal, integrated plans for recovering the entire enterprise and only 7% would characterize their current state of readiness as "excellent," which is defined as having senior-level support and validated, enterprise-wide plans. Fewer than half of the respondents have plans in place for recovering mission-critical systems and some critical business processes; just over one-quarter have plans to recover mission-critical systems and data.

Nine percent described their readiness as "poor," which is defined as "plans may exist but are not updated," and 7% have no documented plans in place. Yet, nearly three-quarters of the firms surveyed indicated that the responsibility for authorizing significant spending on Business Continuity planning projects resides within the executive suite, and most of the remaining companies indicated the Board of Directors bears that responsibility.

Acknowledging that senior executives bear responsibility for driving the issues of continuity and recovery is a positive step, but it is not enough. Executive management must actively sponsor the development of an enterprise-wide, proactive, and formal recovery and continuity program to ensure the long-term security of the organization, and the first step in that process is to allocate sufficient resources. In a sample group in which nearly three-quarters of the companies have more than 10,000 employees, almost one-quarter of respondents have no dedicated, full-time staff allocated to Business Continuity/Disaster Recovery, and another quarter have only one or two people managing the effort. Two-thirds of the companies surveyed have fewer than five people working full-time on Business Continuity.

However, having a nominal plan and a few people in place will be of marginal utility if an incident of sufficient magnitude occurs. Any plan put in place must be *formal*, that is, widely distributed, understood, and rehearsed by the people who will have to assume leadership roles in a crisis. The plan must be *validated*, that is, assessed, tested, adjusted, and reassessed. The validation cycle must be *continuous*.

More than half of the companies surveyed had tested their plans within the previous six months, and nearly one-quarter had tested them within the previous year. But 11% indicated they'd never tested their plans. When a plan is tested, the testing methods themselves must be assessed for appropriate rigor. Nearly two-thirds of respondents indicated that the primary means of ensuring the plans are kept current was by conducting an annual audit. However, just under one-quarter of respondents relied on "occasional spot checks" and 8% indicated they had no method of ensuring their plans were kept current. These are startling results to gather from a sample in which nearly four-fifths of the companies have annual revenues of more than $1 billion.

In the business world, survival is not an accident. It's not fate, and it's not coincidence. It takes organization. It takes planning. Therefore, if an organization has no plans detailing *how* to recover from an unforeseen, catastrophic event, it *may not be able to recover.* A properly planned and deployed Business Continuity Item can help ensure an easier road to fully recovering the enterprise.

THE CHARACTERISTICS

As the Item-by-Item discussion has indicated, an organization can have in place a digital security program that addresses Asset, Entitlement, and Vulnerability Management, Intrusion and Virus Detection, Incident Response, Business Continuity, and Physical Security, and includes fully documented Policies, Standards, and Guidelines, but still not be able to describe that program as "world-class." The definition of a world-class digital security program is that the program must include all of those Items, but each one must be deployed in such a way that it can be described as aligned, enterprise-wide, continuous, proactive, validated, and formal.

During the discussion of the Agenda Items, this Digital Security Overview looked at how major corporations have constructed their digital security programs on an industry-by-industry basis, as well as on the whole. However, when assessing how well organizations have attained the Characteristics of a world-class digital security program, the index scored them with regard to how well *aligned* the digital security objectives and the business objectives were within each organization; whether the security requirements and resulting Items were addressed, understood, and deployed *enterprise-wide;* and whether security-related policies, procedures, and processes were implemented and upgraded in a *continuous* fashion to ensure a timely and effective response.

The study also looked at how *proactive* the organizations were with regard to anticipating and preparing for threats to and vulnerabilities within their systems; the degree to which the firms obtained independent, third-party *validation* of security measures; and the degree to which security policies and procedures could be considered *formal* in terms of their dissemination, implementation, and adherence throughout the organization.

Aggregate scores for the Characteristics suggest that considerable improvement in each area is required for the majority of organizations. Respondents exhibited the highest level of preparedness in terms of having in place formal protocols. This suggests that communicating fundamental guidance on matters relating to information security—policies, procedures, and guidelines that are endorsed by senior staff—is, on average, the study sample's strongest suit. Respondents overall exhibited the lowest level of preparedness with regard to being proactive in their approach, suggesting that there is considerable room for improvement in terms of effectively anticipating potential threats and vulnerabilities to ensure that the confidentiality, integrity, and availability of information are maintained.

Just as they did with respect to the Agenda Items, industry groups exhibited considerable variation in scores within the Characteristics. The Telecom group again achieved the highest scores overall and presented the highest scores for five of the six Characteristics. The Energy group also again achieved the lowest overall scores, scoring below the average for all Characteristics and exhibiting the lowest scores for four of the six Characteristics. The Technology/Media and Automotive/Manufacturing groups presented below average scores in most Characteristics; however, their scores overall clustered near the aggregate averages.

The Financial Services industry appears most skilled in formally communicating fundamental guidance on matters relating to information security, which defines policies, procedures, and guidelines that are endorsed by senior staff, and in terms of obtaining third-party validation of critical security components to confirm that appropriate measures are in place to manage and mitigate risks. This is in line with expectations, given that it is a regulated industry. It also presented above-average scores with respect to having aligned security and business objectives, and having an enterprise-wide view of organizational security needs.

The Life Sciences industry is at a significant disadvantage relative to other industry segments with respect to having validated digital security measures in place to address issues of risk. It also exhibited the lowest industry group scores for maintaining a proactive approach to anticipating threats and vulnerabilities to its information and systems; however, establishing real-time monitoring and continuous updating of all security policies, procedures, and processes to ensure timely response to issues and opportunities appears to be a strength of the Life Sciences industry.

Only when all six Characteristics come together within an Item can an organization be sure it has approached the risks it faces with an enterprise view of digital security. When all Agenda Items are in place, fully aligned with business objectives, continuously assessed and updated, formally documented and distributed, deployed enterprise-wide, proactive in their outlook, and fully validated to appropriate standards, then the organization has achieved the interaction of people, processes, and technology that will enable it to provide a world-class defense of its physical and digital assets.

CONCLUSIONS

Organizations have always taken precautions against physical threats. Today, however, digital threats, whether deliberate or the result of human error, can generate results that are significant, even catastrophic. So many aspects of business depend on digital technology: customer interaction; supplier contact; inter- and intraorganization communication; information collection, storage, and transfer; and automation controls for manufacturing facilities, just to name a few. A digital attack can occur in seconds and can cause consequences that last for months or years. This is why digital security must become an even higher priority for firms of all sizes and in all industries.

The majority of companies surveyed operate in a reactive rather than proactive mode. Whereas such an approach might have been "good enough" in the past and seems adequate in the present, it will be neither in the near future. Not in a future in which terms like "fiduciary responsibility" and "due diligence" are beginning to be used in the same sentence as "digital security." In a future such as the one we foresee, an approach to digital security that is merely adequate may also be considered negligent. Senior management can no longer presume that "someone" in the organization is addressing digital security concerns from a big-picture perspective. The issues and practices discussed in this white paper must become part of the orbit of regard of Chief Executives who wants to see their companies survive and thrive in a globally interconnected world.

The purpose of this white paper has been to present detailed statistics about the current state of digital security in the marketplace, as reflected by ninety-one Fortune 500® firms in North America. Broadly speaking, the results of the Digital Security Overview show that there is considerable difference in the preparedness of individual companies to face and defend themselves against a security incident, but little variation in the level of preparedness among industry groups. This can be construed to indicate that different industries have different security needs and different methods of meeting them or of managing unmet risks. The results also indicate that world-class status is achievable but few of the largest companies in the world are close to achieving it, and the distance of some of them from the pinnacle should be of considerable concern. This study has revealed a high degree of vulnerability across firms and across industries, and closing this vulnerability gap must become a top priority for executive management.

For more information about creating a world-class digital security program or the service capabilities of Ernst & Young's Security & Technology Solutions practice, visit our Web site at www.ey.com/security or call the Security Info-Line at 1-888-706-2600.

DIGITAL SECURITY OVERVIEW
SELF-SCORING DIAGNOSTIC TOOL

A company's ability to defend itself must be proven before an event to know that those defenses will hold during an event. This means there must be a program in place to provide that defense, and that program must be tailored to the unique needs and situation of the organization.

The following tool enables executives to do two things: determine their firm's ability to defend against an attack, and compare their firm to industry peers to determine if theirs would be among the firms able to survive if an industry-wide attack occurred. This systematic assessment can assist executives in understanding where the organization's strengths and weaknesses are, and why they exist. The questions are an abbreviated set of those used in the Ernst & Young 2002 Digital Security Overview. The questions in this tool have been weighted to enable self-scoring according to the Characteristics and Agenda Items of a world-class digital security program.

Instructions: Apply the scores indicated for each answer, following any question-specific directions noted in the shaded boxes. Both Agenda Item and Characteristic should be scored if a Characteristic is noted in the Scoring Box for that question. Please note: *Not all answers are weighted for scoring Characteristics.*

Security Agenda Item: Intrusion Detection

1. Does your company have an Intrusion Detection System?

a) ☐ Yes.	2.00		
b) ☐ No.	0.00		
		Agenda Item	**Characteristic: (None)**
	Score		0

2. What percentage of your Internet and Extranet connections are actively monitored for intrusions?

a) <25%.	0.00		
b) 25%–50%.	0.50		
c) 50%–75%.	1.00		
d) 75%–95%.	1.50		
e) 95%–100%.	2.00		
		Agenda Item	**Characteristic: (Proactive)**
	Score		

3. What percentage of your critical servers are actively monitored for intrusions?

a) <25%.	0.00
b) 25%–50%.	0.25
c) 50%–75%.	0.50
d) 75%–95%.	0.75
e) 95%–100%.	1.00

	Agenda Item	Characteristic: (Enterprise-wide)
Score		

Intrusion Detection Subtotal	
Characteristic subtotal	
Digital Security Overview Subtotal	

Security Agenda Item: Incident Response

4. Which one of the following best characterizes how your organization mitigates internal threats within your networks?

a) Acceptable-use policies and procedures have been established and explained to employees.		0.50
b) Incident response policies and procedures have been developed.		0.75
c) Routine monitoring of employees for misconduct and inappropriate Internet usage.		1.00
d) No measures exist.		0.00

	Agenda Item	Characteristic: (Continuous)
Score		

5. Which of the following would be contacted if your company experienced a major virus problem, an unauthorized network intrusion, or a disclosure of sensitive information on the Internet?

Select all that apply:

a) ☐ Internal computer security incident team.		1.00
b) ☐ An outside vendor that provides computer security incident response.		0.75
c) ☐ The internet service provider (ISP) who advises when network intrusion incidents occur.		0.50
d) ☐ Law enforcement.		0.25
e) ☐ Unsure.		0.00

(Do not add values; assign highest score.)	Agenda Item	Characteristic: (Continuous)
Score		

6. Which of the following best characterizes the level of detail that is provided in your organization's Incident Response Plan?

a) It is a complete document that defines an incident, documents threat alert categories and escalation procedures, details roles and responsibilities, and contains incident scenarios, investigative steps, and system resumption strategies.		2.00
b) It is a summary document that outlines some actions and who to call during an incident.		1.50
c) It is a call list (phone tree).		1.00
d) The organization does not have an IRP.		0.00
e) Unsure.		0.00
	Agenda Item	**Characteristic: (Formal)**
Score		

7. Which of the following statements would you say best describes the level of executive involvement in computer security incidents?

a) Company officers are informed of incidents and are responsible for any resulting business decisions.		1.00
b) Division-level managers are informed of incidents and are responsible for any resulting business decisions.		0.75
c) The computer security incident response team leader is informed of incidents and is responsible for any resulting business decisions.		0.50
d) No formal process exists that requires executive-level involvement.		0.00
	Agenda Item	**Characteristic: (Formal)**
Score		

Incident Response Subtotal	
Characteristic Subtotal	
Digital Security Overview Running Subtotal	

Security Agenda Item: Privacy

8. On a scale of 1 to 5, with 1 being very confident and 5 being unconfident, where would you place your firm with regard to the following privacy practices?

Address all:

a) ☐ We only collect customer's information in accordance with privacy policies. (Aligned)
   1 *(0.50)*, 2 *(0.50)*, 3 *(0.25)*, 4 *(0.25)*, 5 *(0.00)*, Don't know *(0.00)*

b) ☐ We only use or share customer information in accordance with privacy policies. (Aligned)
   1 *(0.50)*, 2 *(0.50)*, 3 *(0.25)*, 4 *(0.25)*, 5 *(0.00)*, Don't know *(0.00)*

c) ☐ We have internal controls and procedures to ensure only authorized persons can access customer data. (Aligned)
   1 *(0.50)*, 2 *(0.50)*, 3 *(0.25)*, 4 *(0.25)*, 5 *(0.00)*, Don't know *(0.00)*

d) ☐ Security procedures are in place to protect personal data from outside hackers or intruders. (Formal)
   1 *(0.50)*, 2 *(0.50)*, 3 *(0.25)*, 4 *(0.25)*, 5 *(0.00)*, Don't know *(0.00)*

e) ☐ We do not release customers' personal data to third parties without the express consent of the consumer or if required by law. (Aligned)		
1 *(0.50)*, 2 *(0.50)*, 3 *(0.25)*, 4 *(0.25)*, 5 *(0.00)*, Don't know *(0.00)*		
f) ☐ We ensure the use of customer information by 3rd parties complies with the privacy policies. (Aligned)		
1 *(0.50)*, 2 *(0.50)*, 3 *(0.25)*, 4 *(0.25)*, 5 *(0.00)*, Don't know *(0.00)*		
(Add all values to ascertain score.)	**Agenda Item**	**Characteristic: (Aligned/Formal)**
Score		

9. Have you completed or are you implementing or assessing the following privacy initiatives? Alternatively, do you consider them unnecessary?

Address all:		
a) ☐ Privacy notice on company's homepage communicating company's online privacy practices. (Formal)		
Completed *(0.25)*, Implementing *(0.25)*, Assessing *(0.00)*, Unnecessary *(0. 00)*		
b) ☐ Privacy notice communicating company's privacy policy for all offline uses of consumer data. (Formal)		
Completed *(0.25)*, Implementing *(0.25)*, Assessing *(0. 00)*, Unnecessary *(0. 00)*		
c) ☐ Privacy notice communicating company's employee privacy practices. (None)		
Completed *(0.25)*, Implementing *(0.25)*, Assessing *(0. 00)*, Unnecessary *(0. 00)*		
d) ☐ Privacy Seal from privacy-seal organizations (e.g., TRUSTe or BBBOnline) posted on company's homepage. (Validated)		
Completed *(0.25)*, Implementing *(0.25)*, Assessing *(0. 00)*, Unnecessary *(0. 00)*		
e) ☐ Appoint Chief Privacy Officer. (None)		
Completed *(0.25)*, Implementing *(0.25)*, Assessing *(0. 00)*, Unnecessary *(0. 00)*		
f) ☐ Privacy dispute resolution program. (Aligned)		
Completed *(0.25)*, Implementing *(0.25)*, Assessing *(0.00)*, Unnecessary *(0. 00)*		
g) ☐ Belong to association that is founded on complying with a set of privacy standards. (Aligned)		
Completed *(0.25)*, Implementing *(0.25)*, Assessing *(0. 00)*, Unnecessary *(0. 00)*		
h) ☐ Independent auditing firm report verifying company is following its privacy policy. (Validated)		
Completed *(0.25)*, Implementing *(0.25)*, Assessing *(0. 00)*, Unnecessary *(0. 00)*		
(Add all values to ascertain score.)	**Agenda Item**	**Characteristic: (Formal, Validated, Aligned)**
Score		

Privacy Subtotal	
Characteristic Subtotal	
Digital Security Overview Running Subtotal	

Security Agenda Item: Policies, Standards, and Guidelines

10. Which of the following are addressed by your organization's IT security plan?

Select all that apply:		
a) ☐ Documents roles and responsibilities/Formal reviews of security controls.		0.125
b) ☐ Information classification and destruction.		0.125
c) ☐ Personnel security and security awareness training.		0.125
d) ☐ Physical and environmental protection.		0.125
e) ☐ Business continuity planning.		0.125
f) ☐ Incident response planning.		0.125
g) ☐ Hardware and systems software maintenance controls/Application software maintenance controls.		0.125
h) ☐ Technical controls (identification, authentication, logical access controls, public access controls).		0.125
(Add all values to ascertain score.)	**Agenda Item**	**Characteristic: (Validated)**
Score		

11. How frequently are your information security policies reviewed for consistency with current business processes and risk strategy?

a) Once a month.	1.00	
b) Quarterly or semiannually.	0.75	
c) Annually.	0.50	
d) When a perceived need arises.	0.25	
e) Rarely/Never.	0.00	
	Agenda Item	**Characteristic: (Aligned)**
Score		

12. To what degree are your information security policies designed to cover the domains defined by ISO 17799, CISSP, Common Criteria, or another recognized model?

a) All necessary policies comply.	1.00	
b) Most necessary policies comply.	0.75	
c) Some necessary policies comply.	0.50	
d) Most policies do not comply.	0.25	
e) No compliance.	0.00	
	Agenda Item	**Characteristic: (Validated)**
Score		

13. How would you characterize your organization's information security policies with regard to being universally deployed, monitored, and administered across the entire organization?

	Agenda Item	Characteristic: (Enterprise-wide)
a) We have attempted universal deployment with no administration/ monitoring of policies.		0.00
b) We have attempted universal deployment with some administration/ monitoring of policies.		0.25
c) We have achieved successful and complete universal monitoring/deployment/ administration of policies.		0.50
d) We have made no attempt at universal deployment.		0.00
Score		

14. How would you characterize your information security policies with regard to being supported by documented procedures and guidelines for all users?

	Agenda Item	Characteristic: (Aligned)
a) They are documented, implemented, and followed.		1.00
b) They are documented; some implemented and followed.		0.75
c) They are documented; not implemented or followed.		0.50
d) Some documented, implemented, and followed.		0.25
e) They are not documented.		0.00
Score		

15. How is policy compliance monitored and administered within your organization?

	Agenda Item	Characteristic: (Validated)
a) It is monitored and administered by a special organizational unit.		0.50
b) It is monitored and administered by select executives.		0.25
c) It is monitored and administrated in ad hoc fashion.		0.00
d) It is not monitored or administered.		0.00
Score		

Policies, Standards and Guidelines Subtotal	
Characteristic Subtotal	
Digital Security Overview Running Subtotal	

Security Agenda Item: Physical Security

16. Which of the following areas are addressed by your organization's physical security policy?

Address all:		
a) Laptop/PC computer security.	☐ Yes *(.625)* ☐ No *(0.00)*	
b) Handling and securing sensitive document printing.	☐ Yes *(.625)* ☐ No *(0.00)*	
c) Handling and securing sensitive mail/mailboxes/mail slots.	☐ Yes *(.625)* ☐ No *(0.00)*	
d) Disposal of sensitive documents.	☐ Yes *(.625)* ☐ No *(0.00)*	
e) We have no physical security policy.	☐ Yes *(0.00)* ☐ No *(0.00)*	
(Add all values to ascertain score.)	**Agenda Item**	**Characteristic: (Enterprise-wide)**
Score		

17. How often do your employees receive training on physical security measures?

a) New hire training.		1.00
b) Annual security awareness training.		2.50
c) Periodic e-mails about security.		1.00
d) Only the security department is formally trained in physical security measures.		1.00
e) No training or e-mailed updates offered.		0.00
(Do not add values; assign highest score.)	**Agenda Item**	**Characteristic: (None)**
Score		

Physical Security Subtotal	
Characteristic Subtotal	
Digital Security Overview Running Subtotal	

Security Agenda Item: Asset Management

18. Which one of the following statements best describes the way your organization currently tracks physical assets?

a) Manually, using a spreadsheet or document to track changes, moves, disposal of assets, and physical inventory.		0.00
b) Automatically, using asset management software to track assets and associated costs.		1.00
c) Partially automated, partially manual.		0.50
d) We do not track physical assets.		0.00
	Agenda Item	**Characteristic: (Continuous)**
Score		

19. Which one of the following statements best describes the way workstation and desktop software upgrades/releases are deployed in your organization (operating system and application upgrades)?

a) Support staff installs software upgrades on an "as needed" basis.		1.00
b) Support staff installs software upgrades per department.		1.00
c) Employees receive automatic upgrades through the network.		2.00
d) Our organization seldom, if ever, upgrades software.		0.00
	Agenda Item	**Characteristic: (None)**
Score		

20. How does your organization inventory the number of PCs in use, types/versions of PC software, available PC disk space, and network IP addresses?

a) The organization uses a comprehensive asset management software package.		2.00
b) The organization uses a software package that inventories some information, but not all asset information.		1.50
c) The organization uses support staff to load software and maintain network information.		1.00
d) The organization uses IT staff to manage network resources and audit PCs for licensed and authorized software.		0.50
e) Other.		0.00
	Agenda Item	**Characteristic: (None)**
Score		

Asset and Service Management Subtotal	
Characteristic Subtotal	
Digital Security Overview Running Subtotal	

Security Agenda Item: Entitlement Management

21. Are the following security solutions currently deployed or is deployment planned?

Address all:

a) ☐ Secure e-mail.	Deployed (0.25)	Planned (0. 00)	Neither (0. 00).
b) ☐ PKI/Digital Certificates.	Deployed (0.25)	Planned (0. 00)	Neither (0. 00).
c) ☐ Centralized User Authentication/ Authorization/Policy Management.	Deployed (0.25)	Planned (0. 00)	Neither (0. 00).
d) ☐ Single Sign-On (SSO).	Deployed (0.25)	Planned (0. 00)	Neither (0. 00).
e) ☐ Web access control/ authorization.	Deployed (0.25)	Planned (0. 00)	Neither (0. 00).
f) ☐ Enterprise Directory Service.	Deployed (0.25)	Planned (0. 00)	Neither (0. 00).
g) ☐ Smartcards/tokens.	Deployed (0.25)	Planned (0. 00)	Neither (0. 00).
h) ☐ Biometrics.	Deployed (0.25)	Planned (0. 00)	Neither (0. 00).
i) ☐ Remote access security.	Deployed (0.25)	Planned (0. 00)	Neither (0. 00).
j) ☐ Wireless security.	Deployed (0.25)	Planned (0. 00)	Neither (0. 00).
k) ☐ Enterprise Security Management.	Deployed (0.25)	Planned (0. 00)	Neither (0. 00).
l) ☐ Security monitoring tools.	Deployed (0.25)	Planned (0. 00)	Neither (0. 00).
m) ☐ Intrusion Detection systems.	Deployed (0.25)	Planned (0. 00)	Neither (0. 00).

(Add all values to ascertain score.)	**Agenda Item**	**Characteristic: (None)**
Score		

22. Approximately what percentage of your IT support staff's efforts are related to user account/password management?

		Agenda Item	Characteristic: (None)
a) 1–5%.	1.75		
b) 5–15%.	1.00		
c) 15–25%.	0.50		
d) More than 25%.	0.00		
e) Do not know.	0.00		
	Score		

Entitlement Management Subtotal	
Characteristic Subtotal	
Digital Security Overview Running Subtotal	

Security Agenda Item: Vulnerability Management

23. Which of the following statements best describes how vulnerabilities of critical systems are communicated to system administrators/security administrators?

		Agenda Item	Characteristic: (Enterprise-wide)
a) The security administrators e-mail daily vulnerabilities to all IT personnel and it is the individual's responsibility to patch the systems.	1.00		
b) The organization separates groups by operating system groups whose responsibility it is to disseminate vulnerability information to the operating system group.	0.75		
c) It is the responsibility of every system administrator to research and patch his or her own system(s).	0.50		
d) We have no communication mechanism in place to alert administrators to vulnerabilities.	0.00		
e) Other.	0.00		
	Score		

24. How often does your organization assess for known vulnerabilities?

		Agenda Item	Characteristic: (Continuous)
a) Daily.	2.00		
b) Weekly.	1.50		
c) Monthly.	1.00		
d) Quarterly.	0.50		
e) Annually.	0.00		
f) Don't know.	0.00		
	Score		

25. In your opinion, which one of the following statements would best describe how effectively your organization manages system vulnerabilities?

a) We have the ability to identify and track vulnerabilities as well as measure compliance.	2.00
b) We have wide-scale deployment of vulnerability tracking and knowledge of all critical infrastructure vulnerabilities.	1.50
c) Vulnerability information is obtained from various sources and administered on a periodic basis.	1.00
d) Vulnerability management is ad hoc and handled by IT or security staff alone.	0.50
e) Vulnerability management has not been addressed.	0.00

	Agenda Item	Characteristic: (Proactive)
Score		

Vulnerability Management Subtotal	
Characteristic Subtotal	
Digital Security Overview Running Subtotal	

Security Agenda Item: Business Continuity

26. In your opinion, which one of the following statements best describes your company's current business continuity/disaster recovery status?

a) No documented plans are in place.	0.00
b) Plans have been developed for recovering our mission-critical systems and data only.	0.25
c) Plans have been developed for recovering critical business processes only.	0.50
d) Plans have been developed for recovering mission-critical systems and some critical business processes.	0.75
e) Integrated plans have been developed for recovering the entire enterprise.	1.00

	Agenda Item	Characteristic: (Formal)
Score		

27. Over the past 12 months, what would you estimate are the number of downtime hours directly related to a disruption?

a) Less than 6 hours.	1.00
b) 6–12 hours.	0.75
c) 12–24 hours.	0.50
d) 24–72 hours.	0.25
e) More than 72 hours.	0.00

	Agenda Item	Characteristic: (Proactive)
Score		

28. When was the last time you tested your business continuity/disaster recovery plans?

a) Within the last 6 months.	2.00	
b) Within the last year.	1.50	
c) Within the last 1–2 years.	1.00	
d) More than 3 years.	0.50	
e) Never been tested.	0.00	
	Agenda Item	**Characteristic: (Validated)**
Score		

29. Typically, what is the PRIMARY means of ensuring that your business continuity/disaster recovery plans are current?

a) Annual audit.	1.00	
b) Occasional spot checks.	0.75	
c) Updates are made following an incident.	0.50	
d) Updating is outsourced to a third party.	0.25	
e) No method in place.	0.00	
	Agenda Item	**Characteristic: (None)**
Score		

Business Continuity Subtotal	
Characteristic Subtotal	
Digital Security Overview Running Subtotal	

Agenda Item Grand Total (Max 45)	
Characteristic Grand Total (Max 30)	
Digital Security Overview Grand Total (Max 75)	

TABLE C.6   Scoring Matrix for a World-Class Security Program

	Aligned	Enterprise-wide	Continuous	Proactive	Validated	Formal	Totals: Agenda Items
Intrusion and Virus Detection							
Incident Response							
Privacy							
Policies, Standards, and Guidelines							
Physical Security							
Asset and Service Management							
Entitlement Management							
Vulnerability Management							
Business Continuity							
Totals: Characteristics							

Endnotes

Preface

1. *The Computer Economics Security Review 2 002*. On www.computer-economics.com/article.cfm?id=356, April 2, 2002.
2. Ernst & Young LLP, *The Security Agenda*®, 2002, p. 7.
3. Ibid., p. 3.

Chapter 1   The Security Frontier

1. Appendix A contains a more complete list of U.S. and international laws and regulations affecting digital security and privacy as it relates to digital security.
2. Please see Appendix A for additional information.
3. Richard Power, "2002 CSI/FBI Computer Crime and Security Survey," *Computer Issues and Trends,* Spring 2002; p. 4.
4. Information Systems Audit and Control Foundation (ISAFC), *Board Briefing on IT Governance.* Available from www.itgovernance.org/boardbriefing.pdf, 2001, p. 4
5. Ibid., p. 9
6. Ibid., p. 7
7. Appendix B provides detailed explanations of specific threats and vulnerabilities.
8. 2002 CSI/FBI Survey, p. 1
9. Ibid., p. 4
10. Ibid.
11. Ibid., p. 6

12. Ibid., p. 9
13. Ibid., p. 10
14. Ibid.
15. In fact, when detected, most attacks are not prosecuted. According to the 2002 CSI/FBI Survey, 77 percent of respondents that had been attacked in the previous 12 months patched the holes in their systems; only 34 percent reported the attacks to law enforcement (p. 20). The most frequently cited reasons for not reporting attacks to law enforcement were negative publicity, the use of the information by competitors, ignorance of the reporting procedure, and a prior decision to seek a civil remedy (p. 21).

Chapter 2   Security Characteristics

All text boxes in Chapter 2 are from the Ernst & Young 2002 Digital Security Overview. The full text of this document is Appendix C in this book.

PART TWO   The Agenda for Action

1. *The Security Agenda*®, 2002, p.3.

Chapter 4   The Security Agenda

1. *The Security Agenda*®, p. 6–7.

Chapter 5   The Three Rs of Digital Security

1. For more information on threats and vulnerabilities, please see Appendix B.
2. Richard Power, "2002 CSI/FBI Computer Crime and Security Survey," *Computer Issues and Trends*, Spring 2002, p. 4.
3. Ibid., p. 10–11
4. Ernst & Young, LLP, *Policies, Standards, & Guidelines*, 2002.
5. *The Computer Economics Security Review* 2002.
6. Ibid.
7. Ibid.
8. *Global Information Security Survey 2002*, Ernst & Young, LLP 2002, Preface
9. *Business Continuity*, Ernst & Young, LLP, 2002.

Chapter 8   Roadmap for Success

1. For a discussion of digital security statistics by industry, please refer to Appendix C.

Glossary of Digital Security Technology

ADMINISTRATION The management of authentication credentials and authorization privileges.

ALERT A message, triggered by an auditing or monitoring program, that describes a circumstance related to network security.

ANKLE-BITER A person with limited computer-related ability and/or knowledge who aspires to be a hacker or cracker.

ANOMALY DETECTION MODEL An intrusion detection model that looks for activity that differs from the normal user/system behavior.

ANONYMOUS FTP A data retrieval system for File Transfer Protocol (FTP) servers that allows access to files by using the user ID *anonymous* instead of the more traditional user ID and password identifiers.

ANTIVIRUS PROGRAMS Utilities that search hard disks for viruses and remove any that are found. Most antivirus programs include an auto-update feature that enables the program to download profiles of new viruses so the application can check for the new viruses soon after discovery.

APPLICATION-LEVEL GATEWAY (FIREWALL) A protective network system configuration that maintains connections and redirects outgoing traffic so that the identity of the internal host server is replaced with the identity of the firewall.

ATTACK An attempt to bypass security controls on a system, or the exploitation of one or more vulnerabilities to cause harm to the target system.

AUDITING Conducting activities to assess the effectiveness of the people, processes, and technology that make up the digital security program. Assessments are conducted to ensure that policy, procedures, and standards are implemented and followed, testing the effectiveness of the digital security program.

AUTHENTICATION Procedures that involve establishing identity through three factors: knowledge (something that you *know*, i.e., a password), possession (something that you *have*, i.e., a random password generator or smart card), and identification (something that you *are*, i.e., fingerprints or a retinal scan).

AUTHORIZATION Procedures that involve assigning permissions to access specific digital assets.

AVAILABILITY The assumption that protected data will remain accessible on demand by authorized users.

BACK DOOR A feature frequently built into systems, programs, or applications that enables developers to have access for the purpose of fixing defects. These intentional vulnerabilities are also known as *trap doors*, and they are frequently exploited by hackers.

BACK ORIFICE A program that was developed as a remote administration tool. When installed on a computer or system, it enables a user, or hacker, to attain full system administrator privileges, including the ability to find passwords and confidential data and e-mail them out of the system.

BANDWIDTH The amount of data that can travel through a given medium.

BIOMETRICS The applied use of digital techniques to authenticate an authorized user's identity by verifying unique physical characteristics, such as fingerprints, voice, or retina.

BROADCAST STORM A network packet or series of packets sent through a gateway to communicate with all subnetworks. It initiates a reply from each system on the subnetworks with the goal of saturating the network and causing service outages. Also referred to as a *kamikaze packet* or *Chernobyl packet*.

BRUTE FORCE ATTACK An attack in which a system is inundated with every possible key or password until the correct one is entered.

BUFFER OVERFLOW The result of too much data being sent to a buffer or holding area in a script or software program. This is generally caused by poor software design or lazy software developers who neglect to properly handle too much or unexpected data as input to a program. This event can cause system crashes and also introduce back door vulnerabilities into a system.

BUG An unintentional flaw or vulnerability in a program or system that causes unwanted or unintended behaviors to occur.

CARNIVORE A system recently developed by the FBI for monitoring e-mail and other Internet traffic.

CENTRALIZED LOGGING A function that enables systems administrators to forward messages from servers to a central system where they can be monitored more effectively. This allows the administrator to maintain a central archive of system logs and proactively scan for errors on systems throughout the network.

COMMON GATEWAY INTERFACE (CGI) A commonly used Web interface that enables servers, clients, operating systems, and programs to talk to each other.

CGI SCRIPTS Strings of code that enable the creation of interactive Web pages. These scripts can be a vulnerability for a Web server, particularly if the system security is porous.

CIPHERTEXT Encrypted data.

CONFIDENTIALITY The assumption that data in any state or location is protected from compromise.

CONTENT FILTERING A procedure for limiting access to undesirable or inappropriate Internet content. Content can be filtered or blocked based on traffic profiles or by site through the use of cataloged URLs.

CONTENT SCANNING A configurable security measure that captures malicious e-mail messages and/or attachments before they enter or leave the organization's systems.

COOKIE A block of text placed on a hard drive by a web site's server. Cookies contain information that assists the server to identify the user's computer. For example, the cookie placed on a user's computer by a web site that requires a login may enable the user to bypass having to login every time he or she visits the web site.

COUNTERMEASURE An action, tool, method, or technique that reduces an information system's vulnerability.

CRACK A tool that enables the user to decode encrypted passwords. It is used by system administrators to discern password-related vulnerabilities, but is more frequently used by hackers.

CRACKER A person who attempts to gain unauthorized access to computer systems with malicious intent.

CRASH The sudden failure of a computer system.

CRITICAL INFORMATION ASSETS Data upon which the organization relies to conduct routine business, for instance, to generate revenue and facilitate communications or transactions. This definition incorporates sensitive and nonsensitive information.

CYBERSPACE The system of globally-interconnected computers and communication systems.

CYBERWAR Information warfare.

DATA-DRIVEN ATTACK An attack in which seemingly benign data is allowed through a firewall and then executed by a user or an action.

DECRYPT To return encrypted data to its original or an otherwise comprehensible form.

DEFAULT PASSWORD A password on a system when it is first delivered or installed.

DEMON DIALER A program that calls the same telephone number repeatedly.

DENIAL-OF-SERVICE ATTACK An orchestrated effort to deny service to an authorized user by overtaxing the resources of the system, thereby rendering it unable to respond to requests.

DIGITAL ASSET Information stored or processed by digital media or devices and the corresponding physical and logical devices used for storage, processing, or transport.

DIGITAL FRONTIER The forward edge of technological impact with respect to organizations' usage of technology and their reliance upon it for day-to-day operations to achieve marketable productivity improvements.

DIGITAL SECURITY GAP The vulnerabilities caused by the exuberant spending in the 1990s on upgraded and open-architecture technologies without commensurate spending on digital security.

DOMAIN NAME The title or name of an Internet host.

DROPPER A file used to conceal and transport a virus into a system or hard drive.

ENCRYPT To change the appearance of a message or data by assigning it a code in order to conceal its meaning from unauthorized persons.

FABRICATION Malicious and deliberate addition of false information into an information system.

FALSE NEGATIVE The indication by a system's security program that no intrusion has taken place when an intrusion actually has occurred.

FALSE POSITIVE The indication by a system's security program that an anomaly or intrusion has taken place when the noted behavior is actually legitimate.

FIREWALL An electronic gate-keeping system that establishes a boundary between systems or networks for the purpose of limiting access and/or traffic.

FULCRUM OF CONTROL The point at which control and containment of a digital security incident becomes critical to the future of the organization. Beyond this point, the situation may be impossible for the digital security team to control.

GATEWAY SCANNING A virus-scanning function implemented at the Internet gateway, enabling the system to contain a virus before it enters the network, and thereby minimizing damage to business critical systems.

HACKER A person who attempts to gain unauthorized access to computer systems.

HACKING The attempt to gain unauthorized access to computer systems, whether successful or not.

HIGH-AVAILABILITY SYSTEM A system that has had technology applied or architecture adjusted to enable the system to operate at a higher level of robustness or to enable the end user of the system to maintain access or recover access to the information in the system in spite of otherwise debilitating events.

HIJACKING The interception of an active session by an unauthorized user. This can occur locally, for instance, if a user leaves his or her computer unsecured and connected, and it can occur across a network or the Internet.

HOLE A system vulnerability that enables security countermeasures to be bypassed.

IN THE WILD Outside of a laboratory. This term is used to describe viruses or other malicious code. A virus laboratory is frequently referred to as a *zoo*.

INFORMATION ASSET Information possessed, whether through ownership or custodianship, by an organization during the process of conducting business.

INTEGRITY The assumption that data in any state or location is protected from unauthorized modification or deletion.

INTERCEPTION Malicious and deliberate capture of digital data in transit between systems or users.

INTERNET SERVICE PROVIDER (ISP) A company that provides Internet access to users.

INTERRUPTION Malicious and deliberate interference in electronic communications that renders networks, web sites, or other electronic systems unusable.

INTRANET A private, internal company network.

IP SPOOFING An attack in which a system uses another system's Internet Protocol (IP) address without authorization or for illicit means.

IT GOVERNANCE The oversight and guidance of information and applied technology within a business and business-related fields by stakeholders, which can include an organization's directors and senior management, as well as process owners and IT suppliers, users, and auditors (from www.itgovernance.org/sponsor.htm).

KEYSTROKE MONITORING The use of specialized software or a device to record every key struck by a computer user, and the computer's response.

LEAPFROG ATTACK The use of a password or user ID obtained in one attack to perpetrate another.

LETTER BOMB An e-mail message that contains malicious code that is activated when the message is opened.

LOGIC BOMB Software that will perform a malicious or destructive action when specific conditions are met. Also called a *fork bomb* or *time bomb*.

LOW AND SLOW A general technique that applies to hackers that conceal or restrict their activities in an attempt to avoid detection by digital security countermeasures. The origin of this term is related to military operations that attempt to avoid detection by the enemy.

MAIL BOMB A large e-mail message or a large volume of e-mail messages that are sent to a user with the intent of crashing the recipient's system.

MALICIOUS CODE Software that is designed to damage a system, application, or data.

MALWARE A term used to describe any malicious software.

MOCKINGBIRD An application that imitates a legitimate system feature or function but engages in malicious behaviors when activated.

MODIFICATION Malicious and deliberate changes to access controls to allow unauthorized privileges or to deny authorized privileges.

NETWORK Two or more computers interconnected to enable communications.

NONREPUDIATION An administrative method of verifying delivery of a message, in which both the sender and recipient are verified.

PASSWORD SNIFFING Analyzing network traffic to discern passwords.

PAYLOAD The action performed during a virus attack.

PERIMETER-BASED SECURITY Applying access controls to all entry and exit points on a network for the purpose of securing it.

PHREAKING Breaking into a telephone network with malicious or mischievous intent.

PIGGY BACK To gain unauthorized access to a computer system by using an authorized user's legitimate connection.

PING (PACKET INTERNET GROUPER) A program that sends test packets to a destination system to ascertain if the system is live.

PING OF DEATH The use of an extremely large ping packet with the intention of causing a denial-of-service attack.

PRIVACY The right of an individual to determine to what degree he or she is willing to disclose personal or other information. When such information is provided to other entities, individuals, or organizations, this right extends to the collection, distribution, and storage of that information.

PROXY A tool that substitutes its own IP address for that of the address of the protected network as traffic passes through a firewall.

REPLICATOR A program that can produce copies of itself.

RISK POSTURE The level of organizational security as aligned with the five threat categories described in Chapter 8. It is the curve that signifies the theoretical capabilities of the organization to mitigate risk (up and to the right of the curve) and the theoretical risk that an organization is accepting (down and to the left) by choosing to take the chance that those incidents will not occur or have impacts that are within the limits of tolerance.

RISK PROFILE The organization's risk with regard to digital security, and with regard to its business objectives.

ROOTKIT A tool that provides a back door into systems for legitimate and illegitimate information-gathering purposes, as well as many other clandestine purposes.

SAMURAI An electronic locksmith or legitimate hacker who performs legal, research-oriented snooping for clients.

SECURITY ADMINISTRATOR TOOL FOR ANALYZING NETWORKS (SATAN) A tool for identifying network system security weaknesses and vulnerabilities remotely.

SCRIPT KIDDIE A person of limited technical knowledge and ability who employs automated tools and exploits known vulnerabilities to disrupt networked systems.

SECURITY FRONTIER The organization's security risk (probability and potential impact of failure) superimposed on productivity (an organization's usage of and reliance on technology).

SECURITY MANAGEMENT GAP The distance between the top levels of management and the security team, which is also the distance between the organization's business goals and the IT department's protection of those goals.

SECURITY RISK The proportionally increased risk a company faces in relation to its proximity to the edge of the digital frontier, based on the higher probability of failure of systems relied upon and the increased impact of that failure when it occurs.

SENSITIVE INFORMATION ASSETS Data, physical or digital, that could, if compromised, pose grave threats to the organization.

SIMPLE MAIL TRANSPORT PROTOCOL (SMTP) The delivery format used by Internet e-mail for transmitting messages between servers.

SMART CARD An access card that contains information that can identify the user.

SMURFING A form of a denial-of-service attack in which the attacker's message impersonates (spoofs) the source address of a PING packet to a network's broadcast address. This contrived PING causes all the network machines to respond simultaneously to the unsuspecting victim network, clogging and potentially crashing the network.

SNARF The act of taking a large document or file with intent to use it with or without the author's permission.

SNEAKER A security expert or legitimate hacker who is hired to test systems' security by breaking into them.

SNIFFER A network monitoring program that captures data as it crosses a network. Network and systems administrators use sniffers for legitimate purposes, such as troubleshooting. Hackers and others use sniffers to steal user IDs and passwords.

SOCIAL ENGINEERING Techniques used by hackers and virus developers to activate viruses or to glean information from unsuspecting computer users.

SPAM Excessive amounts of information sent to a user or a site with the intention of causing the system to crash.

SPOOFING The practice of assuming the identity of another user, for example by using someone else's password or email account.

SECURE SOCKETS LAYER (SSL) An authentication and confidentiality protocol for software applications.

SUBVERSION Modification of intrusion detection operations by an intruder to force the system to produce false negatives.

TERMINAL HIJACKING An attacker takes control of another user's terminal session in progress on a specific machine and is able to send and receive information while that user is on the terminal.

THREAT TO AN INFORMATION SYSTEM Any potential act upon or against the system, of internal or external origin, that is performed with the intention to cause harm.

TIGER TEAMS Groups of computer experts, frequently comprising government or industry experts, that seek out vulnerabilities by testing system defenses.

TIGER A software tool that scans a system and looks for vulnerabilities.

TIME BOMB A software program that requires an action, frequently malicious, to occur at a specific time or on a specific date, or if some specific event occurs or does not occur. An example would be if the author of the program is fired and therefore does not login for a certain number of days, files would be deleted or a virus would be triggered.

TINKERBELL PROGRAM A monitoring program that scans network entry points and alerts system security when traffic from specific sites commences, or when specific login IDs are used.

TRACE PACKET A unique packet used in a packet-switching network. The packet issues progress reports to the network control center as it moves through a system.

TRACEROUTE An information-gathering operation that traces the route of UDP probe packets between the local and remote hosts.

TRIGGERED EVENT A behavior or action caused by malicious code, such as a virus, when certain conditions exist or have been met. An example of a triggered event would be the deletion of all files in a computer's root directory ("C drive") on a certain date or after a specific application has been launched. Also called *sleeper programs*.

TRIPWIRE A software tool used with databases that notifies systems administrators when files' byte count changes.

TROJAN HORSE PROGRAM A nonreplicating, malicious software program that appears to be benign but which enables unauthorized access to information systems without the user's knowledge.

TUNNELING A procedure that viruses use to prevent antivirus software from detecting malicious code.

VACCINE A program that performs a signature check on executable files and alerts system administrators if changes have been made.

VAPORWARE Software that is still in the conceptual or design phase.

VIRUS A self-replicating computer program file that can attach itself to other files or disks and modify them, usually without a user's permission or knowledge. Many viruses, though not all, inflict damage. A partial list of virus types appears below.

- **ANTI-ANTIVIRUS VIRUS** A virus that targets antivirus software.
- **ANTIVIRUS VIRUS** A virus that detects and disables other viruses.
- **ARMORED VIRUS** A virus that contains the capability to disassemble or reverse engineer its code in order to prevent examination or detection.
- **CAVITY VIRUS** A virus that overwrites a part of the file in which it resides but does not alter the file's functionality or increase the size of the file, which enables it to evade detection.
- **CLUSTER VIRUS** A virus that modifies a computer in such a way that, after infection, launching any application will cause the virus to execute.
- **COMPANION VIRUS** A virus that mimics a system file with a similar name, but assigns itself a higher launch priority so that the virus will execute before the default program file.
- **RESIDENT VIRUS** A resident virus infiltrates a computer's memory and does not activate until a trigger event occurs.
- **RETROVIRUS** A virus that continues to infect a system until every backup system and all backup media are infected. The net result of this is that it is not possible to cleanse and restore the system.
- **SELF-ENCRYPTING VIRUS** A virus that encrypts its code differently for each infection in an attempt to avoid detection by antivirus software.
- **SELF-GARBLING VIRUS** A virus that attempts to deceive antivirus software by changing the way its code is structured.
- **SLOW INFECTOR VIRUS** A virus that only infects files when they are created or modified.
- **SPARSE VIRUS** A virus that avoids detection by infecting files only when certain conditions exist, such as file size, or have been met, such as a date that has passed.
- **STEALTH VIRUS** A type of virus that conceals itself from antivirus software by providing a clean but false version of the file the antivirus software is seeking.

VULNERABILITIES Inherent weaknesses in an information system, or weaknesses that are the result of deliberate acts or omissions.

WAR DIALER A software program that dials a range or a list of numbers for the purpose of detecting dial-in access to computer systems. The program records those numbers answering with an electronic handshake, which can indicate an entry point to a digital system.

WORM An independent parasitic software program that replicates but doesn't infect other program files. A worm can replicate on the host computer and stay there, or replicate and send copies of itself to other machines on a network. The damage it inflicts is primarily a service overload that creates gridlock on networks and information systems that can be serious enough to force them to be shut down.

ZOO A group of viruses that have been collected for research purposes.

Index

Access codes, change in, 20
Access control:
  components of, 53–56
  importance of, 64, 103, 111
  incidence response and, 83–84
  operations management, 74
Accessibility, restricted, 62
Accountability, establishment of, 50, 54, 97–98, 105, 108
Account management, 68, 74
Active attacks:
  defined, 84
  incident response, 84–85
Activity log, 24
Activity scanning, 120
Adaptability, importance of, 49
Administration:
  entitlement management, 111–112
  importance of, 120
  incident response program, 87–88
  intrusion/virus detection alerts, 63, 79
  procedures, 54–56
Aligned digital security program, 28–32, 63, 71, 80, 118
Amazon, 144
Antifootprint techniques attacks, 168
Antivirus programs/software, 79, 128
Architecture:
  intrusion detection and, 82

key functions of, 73
  technical requirements design, 73
  technical security, 73
  technology solutions, 73–74
  virus detection and, 82
Architecture team, functions of:
  asset and service management, 105–106
  business continuity plan, 117–118
  entitlement management, 113
  incidence response, 89
  overview, 68
  physical security, 101
  policies, standards, and guidelines, 97
  privacy, 93
  vulnerability management, 109
Asset management:
  components of, 104–105
  Ernst & Young 2000 Digital Security Overview, 188–190
  importance of, 59, 62, 69
  responsibility for, 105–106
  sample scenario, 107
  self-scoring diagnostic tool, 207–208
Asset protection:
  in aligned programs, 29
  critical information, 13, 37
  importance of, 11–12
  managerial responsibility for, 13